WILL THE REAL
KING
STAND UP

WILL THE REAL
KING
STAND UP

MARTIN LUTHER KING, JR., AND MALCOLM X

DR. LARRY L. MACON, SR.

To Dr. Charles Modlin,
Be Blessed & Continue
The Great Work!

Larry L. Macon

Will the Real King Stand Up
by Dr. Larry Macon, Sr.

Cover Design by Atinad Designs.

© Copyright 2013

SAINT PAUL PRESS, DALLAS, TEXAS

First Printing, 2013

The name SAINT PAUL PRESS and its logo are registered as a trademark in the U.S. patent office.

ISBN-10: 0-9912242-2-1
ISBN-13: 978-0-9912242-2-7

Printed in the U.S.A.

"..that government of the people, by the people, for the people, shall not perish from the earth."

President Abraham Lincoln, 1863

"You not only refuse to shoot a man, but you refuse to hate him."

REV. DR. MARTIN LUTHER KING, 1963

*"The Negro revolution is controlled
by foxy white liberals,
by the Government itself."*
Minister Malcolm X, 1963

ACKNOWLEDGEMENTS

This book is dedicated to my wife, Marilyn;
my sons, Larry Lawrence, Jr., and Daniel Lawrence;
my daughter-in-law, Elodie;
and my two beautiful grandchildren,
with love to their future in the shadow of greatness,
Alana Maria and Michael Lawrence.

CONTENTS

INTRODUCTION

We can be sure that one of the most powerful civil rights leaders in the latter twentieth century was a Southern-born, Atlanta-raised Negro named Martin Luther King, Jr. His friends knew him as Michael King. His father had his name changed later during his childhood as he sought to raise this future Protestant theologian in the tradition of the historic black Baptist church. Even today, some forty plus years later, Dr. King's name remains in the annals of history as the purveyor of truth, justice, and love with a work that will not be forgotten anytime soon. The recent dedication of the monument of Martin Luther King, Jr., located in West Potomac Park in Washington, D.C., southwest of the National Mall guarantees his immortalization in history.

We are sure there is still much that has not been revealed about the life and legacy of King. Although his life will be forever immortalized in history, the impact he made on American society is still yet unwinding and is being revealed by scholars like me who are convinced that the whole story of the turbulent 1960s has yet to be fully told.

Hindsight is 20-20, and as we continue studying the civil rights period, it is inevitable we will make additional conclusions regarding that time. It is my intent to provide for the reader and the academic world a further slant on this historic, mystical movement though historians have filled shelves with various tellings and retellings of the life stories of Dr. King and Malcolm X. There have been several theories on who these men really were and what these men really stood for, as well as analysis on what happened in the sixties. Even though I have been teaching the religious ethics of King and X on a university campus, in religious pulpits and among community leaders, I am convinced that King could have been an even greater leader had the community not been "X'd out," or sidetracked and interrupted by the teachings and leadership of his contemporary, Minister Malcolm X.

James Cone, who is known as the Father of Black Theology, among other scholars, argues in his classic writing, *Malcolm & Martin & America*, that Malcolm X became an added incentive for Americans to see the error of racial oppression and deal with King.[1] James Cone argues that Malcolm created an environment where the white ruling class negotiated more readily with King and caused the nation to explore King's many ideas on how to heal the nation of its racism and inequalities. However, I take the position that if Martin and America had never had a Malcolm or an Elijah Muhammad, it would have given King a greater opportunity to explore and understand his nonviolent philosophy. He would have also been able to spend more time directing action and strategy for peace in America and the world. More Americans, especially black Americans, would have been open to hearing and following King's deep theology of non-violence and peaceful resistance. I believe that Malcolm X and his nationalist movement was a national and ethnic distraction and, at times, an interruption from what the real King could have done and accomplished in America with the kind of mental fortitude and religious message that gave him and the nation the moral latitude to take the nation and the world to a place never seen before which was the "Millennium Kingdom of integration on earth," as King phrased it.

In this short journey, I hope to take you on a pilgrimage of not only the life and times of Dr. Martin Luther King, Jr., and Minister Malcolm X, but I want to show you that although both men are important in African-American and American history, one of them stood taller in his leadership exemplified by the appreciation for him demonstrated in today's society. Though Martin Luther King, Jr.'s name included the jargon "king," both men attempted to be kings or leaders in their struggle for freedom. If Malcolm had never existed, history would have been written very differently and perhaps King would still be alive today. Perhaps, he would have been valued differently without the negative connotations given to him by Malcolm as an "Uncle Tom King" which was a direct attack on King's work and personality. The nation may have put greater trust in King, in the absence of a Malcolm and his derogatory displays toward Martin. Our world may have never had a Barack Obama to become the first African-American president some forty years later if King had not had his dream that is held deeply by most Americans today. Obama may not have been president of the United States if many Americans had not embraced an integrationist philosophy.

I invite you to journey with me on a path through the South in a world that may not be too familiar to some today and to continue toward the north of the United States in Pennsylvania and Boston where King's life starts to shift. We will then take our journey through southern cities like Montgomery, Birmingham, and

Selma, and northern cities like Chicago, Detroit, Cleveland, and New York. Afterwards, we will visit the West Coast in Los Angeles where not only Rodney King was beaten, but also Martin Luther King, Jr., was challenged in his dream for a completely integrated society. Consequently, we will not only take these physical journeys, but we must embark upon both spiritual and social journeys, and their effects on the movements nationalism and integrationism.

Last, we will go on a journey into the realm of possibilities of a world without Malcolm X, as well as a world with a Malcolm X who makes a final transition in his philosophy from segregation and nationalism to incomplete integrationism and an inclusive world. We will reason during the journey about what it meant to have a true Islamic faith for black people in America in the earlier sixties that mirrored the kind of orthodox Islamic faith Malcolm held at the end of his life. These are fascinating hypotheses and theories that make scholarly work evolutionary. Perhaps, there will come some young writer behind me who will negate everything I say and formulate new and innovative ideas and thoughts about what might have or might not have been if both King and Malcolm had been equally accepted as kings in the 1960's working together. I welcome the challenge and thought. Enjoy the journey!

1 Cone, James. H. *Martin & Malcolm & America: A Dream or a Nightmare.* Maryknoll, NY: Orbis Books, 1991

WHO WAS THE REAL KING?

When Elvis Presley died, we heard the nation grieve that the "king is dead" and they were referring to the king of rock and roll. Elvis had truly rocked our world with some of his emulations in both the sound and style of black music that he borrowed from Negro singers in step and melody. However, there was another king who borrowed from the black church tradition and rocked this nation's philosophical, moral, and religious foundations with a message of nonviolence. He was none other than Martin Luther King, Jr. We cannot fully understand King's worldview without first exploring his life's developmental stages from birth to death. His life experiences, like ours, determined who he was and informed what he believed, what he stood for, and what he taught others.

It is important that we explore King's earlier life experiences because they help us to understand his later intellectual philosophy of life regarding the solutions he gives to us centering on the problem and solution to racism in America. We know that he was convinced that integration was the solution to racism and segregation. He tells us this in his speeches time and time again. However, perhaps, if Malcolm had never sidetracked America, and, at times, King, or interrupted King on his solutions by challenging America in such a negative way, then King may have been more forceful and persuasive. In particular, black Americans may not have embraced Malcolm's philosophy of what I call "negative nationalism." It is true that some of Malcolm's appreciation for blackness was positive, especially in understanding black culture. But his violent tones, intonations, and undertones may have been negatively given and understood by both blacks and whites. King may have not been what I call "X'd out" in his push for certain integration ideology especially during the time of the Watts riots. It was there that Martin really started settling for a semi-nationalistic stance in what Cone calls a "temporary nationalist philosophy" of both personal and community survival issues.

We are forced to explore King's earlier experiences to understand his later philosophy of the meaning of justice in America and how to achieve it. We must then search out Martin's earlier experiences of violations of justice in America and in his own early and personal life to fully understand his ultimate push for justice for the Negro and all Americans. Of course, there can be no understanding of all of this without a discussion of black and American identity.

Ultimately, America had to face the divide between who she really was and who she claimed to be. The nation claimed Christian theology as her basic religious belief system at the time. However, the nation's claim was different from the nation's action regarding the civil rights of all people. Or at least that idea of Christianity was understood differently by different Americans. Certainly, the Christianity of those Negroes in the deep South was not the same as that of the Ku Klux Klan of the rural South.

America may not have known it at the time, but the exhibition of those qualities and values included crossing lines in a Christian nation. Though she held strong to her initial documents being the U.S. Constitution as the most sacred of all, her practice did not match her creeds. King was eager to point this out to lead America into a clearer conscience of a profession that was consistent with her declarations. America needed to execute full equality for all, with protection of that profession, while at the same time continuing to trust her creeds and documents (which included more than just the Constitution and the Bible) as an outward direction of actions, that ultimately led to the passing of both civil rights and voting rights legislation.

In looking at and exploring the younger King, one must analyze why Martin's answer to violence, drugs, and prison reform was so passively aggressive, and not aggressively violent. King always believed, and challenged his followers, to understand that the nonviolent movement was not just merely a passive movement, but rather it was an aggressive movement minus physical or social violence. It used passive resistance mechanisms such as nonviolent sit-ins to be effective. What a powerful tool, and at the same time, such a misguided and misunderstood philosophy to most Americans.

One of my good aggressive pastoral mentors never agreed with the aggressive-passive or passive-aggressive methods in solving aggressive violent behaviors and acts in America. He refused to march with King because he was aware that if he was approached with violent aggressive behavior by some white person while he was on the protest line, that he would turn the protest out with violent aggressive-active responses. In other words, violence would be the expected result and retaliation for this friend. There were similar people who could not accept King's nonviolent approach to violence. One of them was Malcolm X who thought King's approach was a fool's approach. Malcolm X constantly said that if a two-legged man set his four-legged dogs on him, as they did in Birmingham, then he would do all he could to make sure the two-legged man did not have a leg to stand on. Had Malcolm kept quiet on all his threats regarding a violent America, then perhaps King and America might have remained more focused on pushing Malcolm's philosophical views. After all, I am sure that some biographers of Malcolm have concluded that many of Malcolm's threats were just that–threats. Furthermore, for a man who had so much violent intonation there were many days when he never carried a gun.

I believe the young King may not have been the same King of the latter civil rights period if it had not been for some things shifting in his life. As I read the long list of biographers such as Clayborne Carson, James Cone and others, I am convinced that King had a streak of violence in his character though it did not manifest itself at any time in his life. King was no push over, and he proved it often through direct action in protests. Even as a child, after winning the oratorical contest in school and being reprimanded for not going to the back of the bus, he stood defiantly for ninety miles in action and thoughts. We must realize that violence manifests itself in all kinds of ways and through all kinds of people, and that even we are a reflection of those who are around us. Daddy King, Martin's father, was indeed both violent and threatening. On one occasion, he smashed a cigar in the face of his brother as a symbol of protest to a statement made by his brother. On another occasion, he harshly whipped young Martin and afterwards threatened to whip Martin's young friend who remained outside. I believe this ethic of violence had to have been reflective to young Martin.

Martin Luther King, Jr., expressed a level of violence when during his early life he refused to give up his seat to the white passenger who boarded the local bus during a high school field trip. This took place when King was in high school, and attended an oratorical contest in Valdosta, Georgia, where he took second prize. His victory was soured, however, by the long bus ride back to Atlanta. The bus was segregated, and the black people had to stand so that the white people could sit. On his way back from the contest, he was asked, as all other students, to move to the back of the bus to which young Michael refused. It was his high school teacher who finally encouraged him to move to the back after the bus driver called him all kinds of derogatory names. It was the angry King who exhibited "violent" behavior by standing non-verbally for ninety miles in protest; he refused to even share a seat with his other classmates. Thus, King grew up in a family that encouraged him to notice and respond to injustices.

I see an angry young Michael who admired the violent and angry intonations of his father who constantly and orally aggressively refuted the southern way of segregation. In one incident, the young King saw and heard his father respond violently in language and body tones to a police man who stopped his father while driving and suggested that he had passed the speed limit in the area and called this elderly King "a boy," to which Martin's father responded, "There's a boy; I am a man," pointing to young Michael.[1] One may conclude that the younger King may have envied this violent response since we neither hear nor read of any protest by Martin afterwards.

In none of the biographies do you read of King's disappointment with his father's violent reaction to a shoe store clerk who refused to help him or sell shoes to him when Martin was eight years old. It was Martin, Sr., who refused to go to the "For Colored" section to be served if he wanted to buy shoes, and violently left the store with his angry remark: "If you don't sell me shoes here in this section, you will not sell me shoes in any section," or something to that effect.[2] We can be sure that these and similar remarks of Daddy King, as he was known throughout the area, had to have an impact on Martin. You see this kind of anger in the face of Martin, Jr., during the protest movements. In Ft. Lauderdale, Florida, one can see footage of King, who, like all of us, gets upset when faced with an injustice. I think that is the real King who is often overlooked in biographies and scholarly works.

Though we cannot conclusively argue that young Michael became violent in his response to his childhood white friend's father, who tells him at the age of six that he can no longer come by his friend's house to play because Michael was old enough to understand segregation in the South, King was then made aware through the white father that he is a "colored boy" and the mores in the South hinder whites and Negroes from race mixing. It is Michael, in protest, who runs home to the arms of his grandmother who comforts him by telling him, "You are just as good as anybody."

However, we must accept that although Michael was raised in a stable family, he had seen violence and was familiar with its positive effect for change. He was raised at 401 Auburn Avenue in a large middle-class Victorian house, though just across the street were those poorer sections of the city of Atlanta. His father was the pastor of one of the most influential churches in the city and the nation, Atlanta's well-established Ebenezer Baptist Church, formerly pastored by his grandfather, the Reverend Adam Daniel Williams, who was also an activist in his day. As a child, King was threatened in violence with the "belt" that Daddy King would use not only on his own children, but also on neighborhood kids. I am suggesting that Martin Luther King, Jr.'s early experiences with violence helped him to survive later life experiences.

On the other hand, we cannot dismiss King's understanding of furthering a peaceful life for himself. Martin was given all the correct training of most of the middle class Negroes of his time and era. His father and mother transferred a positive value system to their children and taught them, as most middle class black families, to get a good education that would afford them a level of success in life. Of course, this led to a sense of self-worth and respect for all Americans and, in return, would gain the same from those who reached young black men like Martin. He was taught that if he could remain moral in his dealings with others he would be further accepted by mainstream America. Also, if he carried himself in a businesslike manner that opportunities from whites and black America would be opened to him.

I think that what also helped King to mature into manhood was his relationship with the Ebenezer Baptist Church members. It was no secret that the young King loved his church and the members of his religious institution. His father was not only a pure gospel teacher and preacher of salvation through Jesus Christ, but he was also a social gospel minister who believed in making the good news message applicable in the everyday lives of his parishioners. Martin was known to the entire membership and was loved as the pastor's son. He was a part of the privileged first family whose congregation affirmed him whenever he showed up for church. He often heard those social justice messages that included the love ethics of Jesus Christ and the need to help oneself become a productive member of the Kingdom of God on earth. King's church teachings influenced his praxis in the community as a real leader of black people. He fought for apprehending and attaining justice in his world.

AFFIRMATION ON THE STREET

Martin Luther King, Jr., was constantly being affirmed in his neighborhood. I think he also understood the protection of the streets ethics that kept all kinds of violence away from him. He was both insulated and isolated from the sociological violence of hatred in Atlanta. As long as he stayed on Auburn Avenue he was just fine. Yet, the moment he moved out to what was called "The Five Points" area of downtown Atlanta, he came across physical, social, and psychological violence and racism. It was beyond the streets of Auburn that he would become a "nigger", a "boy", or "colored." It was there that his own father would be considered an uncle to white relatives who were none of his, or his mother would become an auntie when she had no white nieces or nephews. All of them would be faced with those insulting signs: "for Whites Only"and "for Colored Only."

Yet, it was Sweet Auburn, as they called it, that gave to Martin the greatest protection against discrimination. On occasion, he would come out of his house and go up the street and would be greeted by so many people who knew Senior Pastor King's son, Michael. His was not only a religious experience, but a time for him to become familiar with the realms of social, political, educational, and economic empowerment growth of the black community.

It was there on Sweet Auburn Avenue that young Martin experienced the impact of the two largest black denominations in America on Afrocentric communities. He saw and experienced first hand the black Baptist and

Methodist church. After attending his own church, Ebenezer Baptist Church, he would go up the street and hear the prominent black preacher, the Rev. Dr. William Holmes Borders, pastor of the 3,000 seating sanctuary called Wheat Street Baptist Church. There, he and his young friends would engage themselves in a challenge to the community to become more of an activist when injustices were propagated. Dr. Borders was the leader of the church's "Love, Law, and Liberty Movement" which drove buses across the South carrying passengers protesting the injustice being done to them. Towards the end of the Sweet Auburn Avenue was one of the largest African Methodist Episcopal churches in America, the Big Bethel AME church. One can be sure that young Michael saw and heard the bishops of this denomination in all of their regalia, their long ornate robes, and cone-like bishop hats. These two denominations represented the majority of Negroes in America with their large annual conventions and conferences where millions claimed membership.

King also interacted with some of the largest business firms of his days. Auburn Avenue was the main street of Atlanta's African-American business district. John Wesley Dobbs, who was responsible for the Book Depository in the 1940s, said of Auburn, the street was "paved in gold."[3] It was a thriving community. Young

Martin could literally walk up the street and see how a daily newspaper company operated. Young Martin was welcomed inside *Atlanta Daily World* newspaper company whose owner was a member of Ebenezer. Atlanta Life Insurance company prided itself in being one of the largest insurance companies in America having at one time over a hundred million dollars annual operating budget.

When Negroes spoke of Sweet Auburn Avenue, that was what they meant: those churches, clubs, barbershops, shoeshine shops, small businesses, restaurants, and banks were sweet and good at what they did. There on this street were located the three mega economic businesses of black finance: the Citizen Trust bank, mutual Federal Savings & Loan, and Atlanta Life Insurance Company. Auburn Avenue was the black Mecca of Atlanta for blacks. To walk the avenue on any summer evening was to experience the vitality of black life in the city: the sounds of ragtime from the Top Hat club, the smell of fried chicken from Ma Suttons, and the constant sound of street chatter. It was the place where Martin was affirmed as he grew up.

On some occasions, you could hear the singing of Billie Holiday and the playing of Louis Armstrong, Cab Calloway, and B.B. King. Martin Luther King, Jr., known by many of those who owned and operated these businesses, was welcome to stand outside to listen to these historic musicians. Therefore, Martin learned about operating a newspaper company, banking, education, and voter registration, and even having fun experiencing those nightclubs. He saw the importance of the faith-based and religious institutions and the making of secret organizations such as the Masons who held their meetings inside of the large and impressive Mason Hall located on Sweet Auburn.

Malcolm X argued so many times that because Martin Luther King was so privileged, he could never represent the people of the oppressed because he, like John F. Kennedy, was born with a silver spoon of opportunity in his mouth. In other words, King was born in privilege and could not understand what deep suffering was truly all about, and thus, could not lead in the deep ghettos and urban centers of the North. Malcolm argued that since Martin was raised in a middle-class home, where the head of household was the pastor of the elite Ebenezer Baptist Church, he could not be the rightful representative of the group of people whom James Cone, the father of Black Theology, called "the people of the oppressed."

I believe that Malcolm's major internal rift with King

was that Malcolm believed his poor upbringing gave him the right to represent the majority of black people in America who were poor. He was raised poor, an outcast of the privileged by both black and white, not formally educated nor brainwashed by the system. Perhaps, Malcolm felt deeply that he was the rightful heir to the throne of black people and should have been their king, especially when arguing for both human and civil rights of the oppressed. The truth of the matter is that, perhaps, James Cone may be correct to suggest that, perhaps, both of them were kings in their respective social areas and contexts. King was the leader of the South, while Malcolm was both the voice and leader of the North, suggests Cone. However, I think this was an understatement until we begin to see the real Martin Luther King and how he affected America.

1   King, Jr., Martin Luther. *Stride Toward Freedom*, (New York: Harpercollins, 1987), p. 20.

2   Rodgers, William. Martin Luther King Jr., Part 1. *VOA Learning English*. Retrieved from http://learningenglish. voanews.com/content/a-23-a-2005-01-15-2-1-83125947/ 124755.html

3   SweetAuburn.us. *Sweet Auburn Avenue: Triumph of the Spirit*. Retrieved from http://sweetauburn.us/intro.htm

Chapter Two
AN EDUCATED KING

King was a product of his education and academic institutions that he loved, and he greatly appreciated their high academic standards. As a child, King attended Atlanta Public Schools, first David T. Howard Elementary, then Booker T. Washington High School, where he was quarterback of the football team, a violent sport, mind you.

In 1945, at the early age of fifteen, he entered Atlanta's Morehouse College. Martin was a "Morehouse Man" at fifteen years of age and proud of it. He prided himself in sitting in on the Tuesday lectures led by the college's first earned Ph.D. President, Dr. Benjamin E. Mays. King felt the influence of this friend of his father. Mays began to help King understand his true place in the black church. At Morehouse, he would hear his professors and guest lecturers from across America share their theological and sociological slants on the ills of society. During his early years in Morehouse, King began to rationalize the problem of racism as being a structural and systematic concern that needed to be linked to politics and economics in a capitalistic society. He was able to see that this problem was not a problem of mere individualistic thinking, but a social problem that needed to be corrected through government intervention.

At Morehouse College, King was not considered a great student; he was characterized by his teachers as an underachiever. Intellectually, he was dissatisfied by what he perceived as narrow-mindedness in the black southern Baptist church; he was not yet devoted to a life of service to God. He studied sociology and considered going into either law or medicine. At Morehouse, King first read the essays of *Civil Disobedience* by the American scholar, Henry David Thoreau, and was reportedly quite impressed by its emphasis on justice over law. By the end of his time at Morehouse, King had decided that social action was his calling, and that religion was his best means toward that end. He let his father, Daddy King, know about this calling, and gave his first public sermon at the age of seventeen. He was ordained a minister and later served as assistant pastor to his father at Ebenezer Church.

In September 1948, King began his studies at Crozer Theological Seminary in Chester, Pennsylvania, where, unlike at Morehouse, he excelled as a student. Crozer was the first integrated school King attended; he soon became the school's first African-American student body president and later graduated at the top of his class. It was here that he was aroused intellectually, reading everything from theology to secular philosophy, and it was here that he was exposed to ideas which guided his thinking and activities for the rest of his life.

Dr. King read Plato, Aristotle, Luther, Locke, Kant, and Rousseau. Of special interest, were: Hegel, from whom he took an understanding of the challenges of truth and history; Marx, who greatly affected his view of capitalism; Walter Rauschenbusch, who greatly impressed upon him the notion of a social gospel and the church's responsibility for seeking social justice. King accepted Reinhold Niebuhr's pessimistic view of the corrupting influence of organizations on individuals. He kept much of these teachings in mind as he later gained recognition as a leader.

At a lecture at Crozer by A.J. Muste, a well-known American pacifist, King received his first exposure to the ideas of Mahatma Gandhi, which he would later adopt as his own and employ in his nonviolent marches and movement. However, he initially regarded Muste's teaching with some hesitation. Indeed, well into King's initial stage of activism he showed only a partial commitment to the philosophy of pacifism, carrying a gun on occasion during the Montgomery Bus Boycott. Martin kept guns at home in Alabama for self-defense. Whether King began to submit to the principles of nonviolence at Crozer or at a later point, we do not know. We do know, however, that the majority of his intellectual influences were in place by the time he graduated from Crozer in 1951 with a Bachelor of Divinity.

It was there at Crozer Theological Seminary, that he, not only became academically involved with the institution and its fine professors, but it was there that he had experiences with violence that affected his later ability to deal with violence. It is there at Crozer Theological Seminary that he had an encounter with a student who carried a gun and who accused King of playing a college prank on him. While in his dorm room, the student breaks in on Martin and points a gun at him. Martin could have been killed had it not been for another white student who confirmed that Martin did not play the prank and that it was someone else who did. King was face to face with an incident that could have escalated to the point of death.

King undertook the final stage of his doctoral program

at Boston University, to which he had won a fellowship based upon his performance at Crozer. At BU, King clarified his conception of God, adding to it an understanding of personalism, a theological doctrine that stressed the personal nature of God and one's true relationship to God. It was at BU that he was taught the sacredness of human personality as a reflection of God's image. King's later speeches often incorporated these ideas. Although some critics have argued that King's doctoral thesis, titled *A Comparison of the Concepts of God in the Theology of Paul Tillich and Henry Nelson Weiman,* included plagiarized passages, King graduated and successfully received his Ph.D. in 1955 at the young age of 26 years.

AFFIRMATION IN THE CHURCH

Religion was the driving force in King's community. King was moved by his religious faith and driven by his belief in an unseen God. Ebenezer Baptist Church was so much a part of his early life, as it was with so many other youth in the community. His church was, indeed, among the true historic black churches of his day. Daddy King led his family to embrace the Baptist Denomination. King was fascinated by his early experience with the church: the choirs singing anthems, hymns, and gospel music; the ushers standing at guard for the waiting congregation to enter the facility and be escorted to their seats; the deacons and trustees who walked into the service with their business suits and stern faces; his mother, Mrs. Alberta King; and most of all, the leader of the church, the elder and pastor, his dad, the Rev. Dr. Martin Luther King, Sr., who seldom smiled during the worship service.

Daddy King was an interesting person as well. He was born on December 19, 1899, and was first named Michael. Daddy King's father, James Albert King, had been a sharecropper near the small town of Stockbridge, Georgia, outside Atlanta. Like most sharecroppers, he had worked hard and earned little money. King, Sr., the second of ten children, left Stockbridge for Atlanta at the age of sixteen, with nothing but a sixth-grade education and a pair of shoes.

In Atlanta, he worked odd jobs and studied, and slowly developed a knack as a preacher. While preaching at two small churches outside of Atlanta, he met Alberta Christine Williams, his future wife and Martin's mother. She was a graduate of Atlanta's Spelman College, had attended the Hampton Institute in Virginia, and had returned to Atlanta to teach and play the piano. Her father, the Reverend Adam Daniel Williams, was the pastor of Atlanta's well known Ebenezer Baptist Church.

After King, Sr., and Christine Williams married, they moved into the Williams' home on Auburn Avenue, the main street of Atlanta's African-American business district. After several years had passed, her father asked King, Sr., to serve as assistant pastor at Ebenezer, which he did. When the senior pastor died of a heart attack in 1931, King, Sr., took over as the new pastor and continued in the traditional style of black worship with the enthusiastic singing and whooping, loud, exciting, singsong preaching style. Martin Luther King, Jr., later explained how he did not initially like the emotional preaching style of his father and preferred an intellectual presentation which is what he delivered in his own ministry, before moving closer to the more emotional style later in his life. Early in Martin's life he became fascinated by language and the power of words and sound. He wanted to "get some big words" when he got older, therefore, he didn't take pleasure in the traditional "whooping" and "hollering" of preachers like his dad.

King, Jr., his brother, and his sister were born into a financially secure middle-class family, and received a better education than the average child of their race. King's recognition of this undoubtedly influenced him in his decision to live a life of social protest, wanting to extend the opportunities he had enjoyed to all blacks. Because of his father, King had a model of courage through the black church. King, Sr., involved in the local chapter of the National Association for the Advancement of Colored People, or NAACP, had led a successful campaign to equalize the salaries of white and black teachers in Atlanta.

The elder King's foundational institution was Ebenezer Baptist Church which supported their pastor in all endeavors from worship to social protest. The songs of protest were used on the streets of protest. Later, Martin Luther King, Jr., would use them at the Dexter Avenue Baptist Church. The younger King's one and only pastorate would duplicate the same kind of mission as his father's church in not only presenting a gospel message of redemption, but in direct action through protests which often included the use of black church spirituals.

One of the most important developments in King's life in Boston that transferred to Dexter in Montgomery occurred outside the classroom. In 1951, he met Coretta Scott, his future wife, a fellow Southerner who was studying voice at the New England Conservatory of Music. Initially, Coretta had hesitations about being involved with a minister and one who looked like Martin —dark and short, but King was forthright in his courtship. On their first date, he told her she had all the qualities he sought in a wife. They were married on June 18, 1953, by Martin Luther King, Sr., on the lawn of Coretta's family home in Marion, Alabama.

AFFIRMATION IN HIS NEW COMMUNITY

When King finished his coursework at Boston University, he took the position as pastor of Dexter Avenue Baptist Church in Montgomery, Alabama. It was an established church of well-educated, middle-class Negroes with a history of civil rights protests. At first, King had mixed feelings about the pastorate and considered work elsewhere, possibly at a place in which he could teach in a college or university as well as preach. However, his salary was the highest black ministerial salary in town.

Montgomery, as the old capital of the Confederacy, was one of the seats of racism in the South. It probably made sense to King to test his theories on the need for a social gospel message with those in Montgomery.

At the end of 1955, Coretta gave birth to a baby girl, Yolanda Denise, whose arrival may have contributed to the couple's decision to stay.

On December 1, 1955, a black woman named Rosa Parks refused to give up her seat on a Montgomery bus. The bus company's policy dictated that black passengers fill seats from the back and white passengers fill seats from the front. Where the sections met, blacks were expected to give their seats up to whites. Discrimination and racism on buses were strengthened by the attitude of the all-white driving staff, who were known to harass black passengers verbally, and sometimes physically.

Rosa Parks was an important person in the protest. She worked as a tailor for a Montgomery department store and a member of the local chapter of the National Association for the Advancement of Colored People (NAACP), having served as its secretary since the 1940s. It was her unplanned and steady act of courage on that day which caused a chain of events to unfold that concluded with a United States Supreme Court decision prohibiting bus segregation and King's rise to national prominence.

The driver, whom Parks challenged, had her arrested, and she was released on bond. Her relationship to the NAACP and the affirmation of the black community meant that the case attracted instant citywide attention. When she was arrested, a group of community ministers and leaders met immediately and planned a boycott. Meanwhile, the NAACP lawyers took on her court case, believing they could possibly win and they could take the issue to the Supreme Court, considering their recent victory in the case of *Brown v. Board of Education of Topeka, Kansas.*

The organizers of the boycott were from other black groups, such as the Women's Political Council which met in the basement of Dexter Avenue Baptist Church, which King had offered as a site. The group developed three demands for the bus company: that seating be available on a strictly first-come, first-serve basis; that drivers conduct themselves with greater respect to black passengers; and that black drivers be hired for predominately black routes. There was no call for integrating seating. To secure these demands, it was agreed that no blacks would ride the buses on Monday, December 5th.

On the first day of the protest, hardly any blacks rode the buses. Afterwards, nearly 20,000 blacks supported and affirmed the action. Because blacks constituted the majority of the bus system's customers, many buses drove around empty. Because of the black community's eagerness to agree with the boycott and because of the bus company's refusal to submit to the community leaders there was held a second meeting on the afternoon of the boycott to plan an extended protest. The group named itself the Montgomery Improvement

Association, or MIA, and elected and affirmed Martin Luther King, Jr., as their president. King was confirmed as their new leader in the community and received their support. Though only twenty-six years of age, he showed great promise as a leader. He was new to the city of Montgomery and was new to the old local politics. From the beginning, and throughout the most challenging of violent events of the lengthy boycott, King never failed to emphasize the protest's foundation in Christian principles. Though the protesters might be the victims of violence, black protesters would engage in no acts of violence whether verbal or physical themselves. They were determined that they would "turn the other cheek" as the Bible suggested. This set the tone for all of King's future campaigns and protests.

The boycott lasted over a year, and changed both King's life and the city of Montgomery. King became the target of numerous telephoned threats and a few acts of violence. His house was bombed. He was arrested under false pretenses and harassed. He was sued for various reasons, and yet, he became very well known and loved by the masses.

The most affecting experience King had was the night of the boycott where he had a religious manifestation in his mind and spirit where he was approved by God. As

King described it, he had come home from a meeting and his wife was asleep; the phone rang, and when he answered it, an anonymous caller threatened his life suggesting that he commit suicide. After that, he could not sleep. He made some coffee and sat in his kitchen. For a moment the path before him seemed absolutely impossible. Then, while praying aloud, King felt the presence of God. It was very sudden and very intense, and he had never experienced anything like it before. King explained that this experience helped him to no longer fear the danger of the boycott, the threats on his life, nor the protest actions that followed.

The City of Montgomery ultimately changed. To follow up on the boycott, the black community formed a network of carpools and informal taxi services. Some white employers were forced to transport their black employees themselves. Many blacks walked long distances to work each day. The boycott quickly began to hurt the businesses of city store owners, not to mention that of the bus company itself; it was losing the majority of its income. However, instead of accepting the demands of the MIA, whites attempted to end the boycott by other means through a series of bombings of churches and private homes, and through the courts. The MIA compensated drivers who transported boycotters whom the city sued for running an illegal transit system. While King was in court defending the MIA against the injunction, news arrived that the Supreme Court had ruled in favor of Rosa Parks, and had made it illegal to segregate on buses in Montgomery.

This ended the boycott, and on December 21, 1956, over a year after Rosa Parks' refusal to relinquish her seat, King joined Ralph Abernathy, his assistant, and other boycott leaders for a first ride on a desegregated bus. Violence continued after the boycott: more homes and churches were bombed, and some white people threw stones and shot bullets at the buses. However, no matter how small the victory was at the local level, it marked a national success for Martin Luther King and for the cause of African-Americans as a whole. King's prominence was raised to a national level and was later recognized by the nation.

After the Montgomery Bus Boycott, King's life mission was set. He was a civil rights leader for the rest of his life, using the academic tools he had learned in colleges and the university which taught him both his strategies and his goals. It was on August 28, 1963 where he and his followers won another major victory at the March on Washington. However, we can't dismiss the fact that in the late 1950s both time and conditions allowed him a time of preparation, trial and error, partial victories, and many lessons. Dr. Martin Luther King's education began to pay off and he was collecting social and political dividends.

Chapter Three
THE VOICE OF AN ANGRY KING

NATIONALISM IN HIS BLOOD

Malcolm Little, who later became known as Malcolm X, was proud to be called the "Angriest Negro in America."[1] He sometimes acted more like a dethroned king. In his mind, I believe he thought he was born to rebel against America's racist system. He thought, perhaps, he should be "king" of an anti-racist world.

As a child, he heard his father reject the American side of their identity and affirm their proud African heritage. He became both vocal and verbal in his aspiration to lead blacks into such liberation through his loud, aggressive, and sometimes, abusive language and messages. He argued vehemently that America did not want integration of blacks and whites, and that blacks should never want any affiliation with whites in America. He understood the history of racism in America with its

244 years of legalized slavery and 100 years of segregation, and was sure that white America would be destroyed for its political and economic injustice that led to social disenfranchisement. He thought that there was no other way out for blacks than to totally separate themselves from the system; for Malcolm, it was an urgent situation.

How did all of this rage, anger, and what some have described as hatred, manifest itself within this man of many gifts? I believe it started in his childhood. Malcolm had nationalism implanted in his blood. If there is such a thing as "nationalistic blood transfusion," young Malcolm received it during his early life. To understand the nationalist view and the effect it had on Malcolm X, we have to go back to his early life.

Malcolm Little, son of an African-American Baptist preacher, Earl Little, was born in Omaha, Nebraska, on May 19, 1925. Malcolm's mother, Louise Little, was born in the West Indies and was light-complexioned. Her mother was black, but her father was a white man. Earl, an extremely dark-skinned man, sent a telegram to his parents in Georgia: "It's a boy, but he's white, just like his mama." Malcolm looked like his mother and paternal grandmother with blue-green eyes and reddish, ash-blonde hair with a tinge of cinnamon. His father called him "an albino" because he was so light-complexioned, while his brothers called him "high yellow" and sometimes, "a freak of nature." While his father was from Reynolds, Georgia, his mother was from the Caribbean Island of Granada, and Malcolm believed that his mother was conceived in rape by her Scottish father who was a plantation owner and who also violated his maternal grandmother. Malcolm later informed the world of his hatred for every drop of white blood that flowed through his body.

MALCOLM INTRODUCED TO VIOLENCE

Malcolm was introduced to violence early in life. He saw his angry father physically abuse and beat his mother on more than one occasion. This six foot tall, very dark complexioned Negro had been married twice. He and his first wife had three children, Ella, Mary, and Earl, Jr. He had six children by Louise, his second wife. Earl was the epitome of "the angry black man" in America. However, Louise loved Earl and Earl loved his beautiful light-skinned wife. Earl was also brutal to his children, whipping all of them except for Malcolm whom he favored. Malcolm was seldom whipped for his wrongdoings probably because his father was conflicted with his own self-identification. Earl favored Malcolm's light skin, while Louise was in conflict with her light skin and favored her other children's dark skin. Louise whipped Malcolm more than she did her other children. Malcolm learned to stay away from his mother.

It is Malcolm who saw both the controlled and angry side of his father. Earl was an itinerant Baptist preacher who went from church to church ministering in the traditional black preacher style. He pounded his hand on the pulpit, yelled and screamed his messages, sweating himself into a kind of frenzy filled with emotionalism. Malcolm was both confused and amazed as he watched his father jumping and shouting at church. Earl and the Baptist congregations that he preached to lost Malcolm's respect for the traditional black church while his brother, Philbert and others would laugh at this kind of worship experience, which was entertaining to them.

It is the other side of Earl that Malcolm appreciated and affirmed which he saw throughout the week. While Earl expressed himself deeply and emotionally in the black Baptist denominational pulpit on Sundays, he attended the Marcus Garvey Movement meetings during the week and expressed a kind of intellectual ministry style. Malcolm took pride in seeing this side of his father. He was smooth, controlled, and yet, tough. He chose his words wisely to promote the message he intended to relay to the Universal Negro Improvement Association (UNIA), an organization started by the black liberationist, Marcus Garvey. Though Earl was still angry about his plight in a racist white America, he expressed it in an intelligent and a more gentle, rational way, as Malcolm interpreted it. It was this black consciousness group that raised the issue of discrimination of blacks in America and the world, while at the same time proposing solutions for white supremacy over blacks. Therefore, young Malcolm was able to see anger and violence both in his father and mother as he was being nurtured as a child.

Eugene Victor Wolfenstein, in his writings, *Victims of Democracy: Malcolm X and the Black Revolution*, does an excellent presentation detailing the three major incidents that promoted Malcolm's earlier years of rage, anger, and violence that led to his nationalistic views and philosophy. They include an incident with the KKK, the negative response of his eighth grade teacher towards a black Malcolm, and the death of his father. However, Alex Haley's *Autobiography of Malcolm X* is a better resource in gaining an understanding of what those incidents meant to Malcolm as he interpreted their effects on his life. It was these early incidents in Malcolm's life that helped him to conclude that the white men were the devil. These evil and most unfortunate happenings developed the Malcolm of Nationalism whose views opposed the King of Integration.

RAISED IN A VIOLENT NEIGHBORHOOD

Along with the experience of being raised in a violent home of aggression with expressions of violence and seeing his father express himself in verbally aggressive ways in the church and UNIA meetings, Malcolm experienced violence first hand in his neighborhood. At the age of four, his family was victimized by the Legionnaires of Lansing, Michigan, a group of white supremacists who hated blacks who attempted to integrate their neighborhood. Earl, his father, bought a home in a predominantly white neighborhood.

Members of this white supremacy group attempted to burn their family house down, while the family was sleeping in their beds. Malcolm woke up in the middle of the night both terrified and confused, and vividly recalled how he had been suddenly snatched awake into a frightening confusion of pistol shots, shouting, smoke and flames. His father woke up and ran to the front porch with his gun and shot towards the men while shouting defamatory remarks at those who set the fire. The men ran away and Malcolm was left on the porch in his undergarments traumatized at the event and angry with the white racists.

Malcolm, as an adult, remembered how they tried to escape before the house collapsed. The family found themselves outside in the night crying and yelling at the injustice brought upon them by the Legionnaires. This was for Malcolm his earliest vivid remembrance of being in what he later called "a terrifying and confusing nightmare."[2] Young Malcolm and his family had no problem concluding from that point on that the white man, and thus all of white America, was indeed a powerful and evil force that blacks in America needed to fear and hate. For Malcolm, this was Christianity at its worst, because these so-called "good Christians" were Ku Klux Klan members.

The second major incident that led to Malcolm's conclusion that violence ought to be the appropriate response to an evil white society occurred when Malcolm was six years of age when his father was found dead under a street car. Malcolm believes he was thrown under by the "Good White Christians," the KKK. Malcolm's family was told that his father's death was an accident. Later, the insurance company representative ruled it a suicide, thus voiding Earl's life insurance policy which relegated his family to a life of poverty. Malcolm concluded it was murder by the white supremacy organization.

The third major incident that affected Malcolm's life was what some biographers have called "The Ostrowski Episode" where Malcolm, in his eighth grade class, was asked about his future. Malcolm was a black student in an all white school and was asked by his teacher, Mr. Ostrowski, what was it he wanted to become in life, to which Malcolm responded, "a lawyer." Malcolm was admonished by the teacher to be realistic and to desire a profession suitable to "niggers." The teacher suggested Malcolm become a carpenter like Jesus.

Though Malcolm was young, he was aware of the teacher's attempt to dehumanize him and segregate him from the other students psychologically. Young Malcolm was so outraged that he became reclusive in the classroom and school to the point of muting all conversations that he held with faculty, staff, and students of the school. While Malcolm thought he had integrated into white mainstream through being accepted in this white school, he clearly understood that physical inclusion did not guarantee social and psychological inclusion. Malcolm was aware of how racism looked, felt, and moved. Mr. Ostrowski was finally exposed and Malcolm believed his teacher was a racist. The young Malcolm had placed his teachers and classmates in the same category: racists in a racist society. He was angry, frustrated, resentful, and ready to move on in his life. He was pushed from the white world, and then as he said, "I changed inside." He requested to live with his half-sister, Ella, in upper Roxbury outside of Boston away from all white people. He was now a nationalist without formality.

MALCOLM AND THE STREETS

As King was affirmed in his neighborhood that led to his nonviolent philosophy, so was Malcolm affirmed in his neighborhood of violent attitude, rhetoric, and behavior. Upper Roxbury where the gentler, kinder African-Americans lived may have created a different personality and given another perspective to Malcolm. He could not remain in the Upper area of middle-class bourgeois. It was there that middle class blacks attended their quiet traditional churches and met with blacks similar to those who lived on Sweet Auburn. However, Malcolm chose the street life and hustler's community called, Lower Roxbury. It was there that Malcolm would express his anger and see violence first-hand in the streets. It was there that he was truly trained in retaliation and the creation of a battalion of blacks who felt they had little to live for and much to risk in the streets. It was his outlet from a complicated life.

Malcolm was there in the Boston area at the time of the Great Migration where millions of blacks left the South to move to the "Promised Land" of the North, only to find their dreams dashed and dampened by a life of crime, drugs, pimps, and poverty, especially for the black male who left the South with a promise that he would return to those southern urban and rural areas to bring his family up north to a life of prosperity. Because of the estimated 2.5 million who moved to the North during the Great Migration, the cities could not accommodate the black masses. There were not enough jobs, housing, and even churches to go around to support the great masses. Churches created out of abandoned storefronts had to be used in place of the beautiful, small, gothic style Negro churches in the South. The streets became outlets for discontented people, and the lifestyle of black males became less than favorable. Some of them chose to be a part of street gangs, pimping women on the streets, selling drugs, and violence by way of robbery and thievery at any cost. This street life and its ethics became their survival mechanism in the newfound ghettos of lower Roxbury.

Malcolm's first line of work was washing dishes on a Boston to Washington train line. Afterwards, he was promoted to selling sandwiches as a porter on a Boston to New York train line. He was mesmerized by the wealth and energy of New York, especially Harlem's Savoy Ballroom and Apollo Theater. After being fired for being too forward towards customers he sold sandwiches to, it was not long before Malcolm found his way into the ghetto and street life of lower Roxbury. At the time, he knew it was time to take off his old fashioned zoot suit and put on his pimp suit and work the streets of his new home. He became attached to a street gang led by a local thug and number man named West Indian Archie who was raised in Grenada. It was this gang leader, numbers pusher, pimp acting, gun-toting black man who taught Malcolm the ethics of the street. He taught him the worst of black manhood although Malcolm believed it to be manhood at its best. West Indian Archie promoted the negative side and behavior of Malcolm Little.

Malcolm was happy to work as a day waiter at a Harlem bar called Small's Paradise after he moved to Harlem. He made a good impression on the customers and on his employers, and learned many hustling techniques, the ethics of the Harlem underworld, and the history of the neighborhood. He took long walks with the old timers. With his tips, Malcolm began to invest much money in the numbers racket in Harlem. He learned the names and faces of the old numbers runners as well as those who were recently employed as black gangsters.

Malcolm also met a variety of pimps, including one known as Sammy the Pimp, who soon became his best friend and confidant.

Malcolm took on a variety of odd jobs in Harlem. For six months he handled gambling slips for the illegal numbers system. Then, after working in a gambling house, Malcolm worked for a prostitution house, steering white people from downtown to the different places where they were sexually engaged with black and white prostitutes.

However, Malcolm's street life soon caught up with him. In 1945, Malcolm was accused of robbing a gambling game ran by Italian mobsters. He began fearing for his life just walking the streets of Harlem. He quit his numbers job and began importing bootlegged liquor from Long Island for a Jewish businessman. He liked the work, but his boss disappeared suddenly after a scandal involving the bootlegging business.

Malcolm himself began to increase his own play of the numbers, placing large bets with West Indian Archie. He was known for his photographic memory, which meant he did not have to write down any of the bets on paper. Malcolm, one day, ran into problems when West Indian Archie accused him of collecting winnings on a bet he had not placed. Malcolm insisted he had placed the right number on the bet, and according to the code of street ethics, Malcolm nor Archie could back down. West Indian Archie submitted to Malcolm's memory and gave Malcolm the money. Archie changed his mind and gave him until the next day to return the money that he had reluctantly given to him. Malcolm got intoxicated on various drugs and woke up long after the deadline given by Archie. He returned to Harlem, where he ran into West Indian Archie at a bar. A confrontation ensued, and Archie humiliated Malcolm but did not shoot him.

The next day, Malcolm punched a young hustler in the face, was almost stabbed, and was searched by the police. Consequently, the police, the Italian mob, and the hustler Malcolm had punched, along with Archie, were all out for Malcolm's life, and he felt more threatened than ever. Just as Malcolm thought he was going to get shot, Shorty, his new friend, picked him up and took him back to Boston.

In Boston, Shorty and Ella, his half sister, were amazed at the changes they saw in Malcolm. He was quite edgy and short-tempered. He profusely used profanity that he had learned from the hustling community. It took Malcolm a few weeks to unwind from the tension and fear he met during his situation in Harlem. At first, all Malcolm did was continue sleeping, smoking marijuana, and playing records. He then began to participate in drugs again, in particular cocaine which affected his thinking. Simultaneously, he talked excessively to Shorty and Sophia, his white girlfriend, about future plans. He remained close to Sophia and depended on her for money and was surprised at how much abuse she took from him. Sophia was married and her husband was often on the road on business, which enabled Malcolm to see Sophia frequently. Shorty began dating Sophia's seventeen-year-old sister.

To sustain himself and his drug habits, Malcolm decided to find a new hustle. Using his reputation as a ruthless and dangerous thug, he put together a burglary ring consisting of himself, Shorty, and a light-skinned black Italian man named Rudy. They included Sophia and her sister to search out white neighborhoods without arousing suspicion. Usually, the women visited a home, knocked on the door posing as sales persons and persuaded the homemaker to give a tour of the layout of their homes. The women then returned to the ring and described what they saw in the house. The men then returned to the house at night to commit robbery. Shorty and Malcolm became nighttime burglars, while Rudy became the driver in the getaway car. Initially, this was a lucrative and successful venture until they were caught.

Malcolm's slip up occurred when he was high on cocaine. He found Sophia and her sister in a black bar with a white man who was a friend of Sophia's husband. Malcolm walked over to the bar counter and addressed the two women intimately, exposing his relationship with Sophia. Later, the friend and Sophia's husband went on the hunt to find him. When police arrested Malcolm in a pawnshop, he gave himself up peacefully. They took him and Shorty to court. In court he was charged not only with stealing, but the judge attempted to get Sophia and her sister to accuse both Malcolm and Shorty of raping white women. Even though they would not, Malcolm and Shorty were penalized for having relationships with white women. Malcolm was repeatedly cross-examined on the origin and nature of his relationships with the women instead of on the crime of burglary with which he was charged. Malcolm was sentenced to ten years in state prison. Malcolm, who was then angrier than ever, entered into jail as an angry black man. Yet, he did seven and a half years and got out early on probation.

1   Caffrey, Hugh. Malcolm X - "They called me the angriest Negro in America". *The Socialist*. Retrieved from http:// www.socialistworld.net/doc/1594

2   Wolfenstein, E. Victor. *The Victims of Democracy: Malcolm X and the Black Revolution*. (London: University of California Press, 1981), pg. 88.

Chapter Four
MALCOLM: A SELF-TAUGHT KING

Malcolm's time in a Massachusetts State prison was a period of intellectual growth and religious turmoil and conflict. Suffering from drug withdrawal and a fierce temper, he was placed in solitary confinement and nicknamed "Satan." He met Bimbi, a confident black prisoner whose speech commanded the respect of guards and inmates alike. Under Bimbi's instruction, Malcolm began to think outside the hustler mindset of Roxbury and Harlem. He made use of the small prison library, refined his English, and channeled his rage into rational arguments.

His interest in learning how to read and write increased because of Bimbi.[1] This inmate took control over all conversations he held with Malcolm because of his huge knowledge. This made Malcolm kind of jealous and motivated him to start learning. He started to copy a whole dictionary and learned many new words. As his learning increased, so did his reading of books. Malcolm found something to focus on and believed that nobody else got more out of going to prison than he did.

In 1948, Malcolm moved to Norfolk Prison Colony, where there was less violence, less surveillance, and more freedom where inmates could indulge in study and debate. At the large library there, he immersed himself in subject after subject, in book after book, including history, religion, literature, biology, and linguistics.

Malcolm first heard about the Nation of Islam (NOI) from members of his own family. There were those living in Detroit while others remained in the Boston area. He became a devout follower of the Nation of Islam led by the Honorable Elijah Muhammad. He accepted their dietary law and gave up pork at his brother Reginald's request who identified it as forbidden food. Later, seeing this decision as his first step toward becoming a Muslim, Reginald told Malcolm about the Nation of Islam's spiritual leader, Elijah Muhammad, whose central teaching revolved around the fact that all whites are devils.

While deciding whether or not to convert, Malcolm thought of all the white people he had ever known. He remembered the social workers who split up his family, the teacher who discouraged him from becoming a lawyer, and his customers when he worked as a porter and a pimp. He also thought about the white policemen, judge, and guards who worked together to lock him away in prison. Every one of these people, he reflected, had done him harm. He began to undergo an overwhelming change and to feel that the sin and guilt of his past had prepared him to accept the teachings of the Nation of Islam.

Malcolm accepted the Nation of Islam's principles and guidelines. According to Elijah Muhammad, the first humans that inhabited the earth were black, living peacefully under Allah in Mecca. Then, a mad scientist named, Yacob, unleashed an evil race of white people on Europe who conspired to abuse non-whites for 6,000 years. Elijah Muhammad taught that black people were stolen from Africa, sold into bondage, and finally brainwashed in America. He accepted the teaching that white people forced them to accept the names, customs, myths, and gods of their masters. Now, however, Elijah's teaching included the fact that white civilization was destroying itself and black people. Malcolm later on wrote to Elijah Muhammad daily and received direct teaching from Muhammad. He learned how to pray, which Malcolm said was one of the most humbling experiences for him.

To improve his writing skills, Malcolm slowly copied out the whole dictionary longhand, starting with the word "aardvark." With an expanded vocabulary, he began to read until he was staying up half the night studying in his cell. He said that reading awoke in him "some long dormant craving to be mentally alive." Malcolm soon embraced a religious system of beliefs that has Africa at its center. From other sources, he learned that the first men and the great early civilizations were African, that the pharaohs were Africans, and that the great Western storyteller, Aesop, was an African. The horror of slavery and the bold nineteenth-century revolts of Nat Turner and John Brown deeply impacted him. Studying the anti-British resistance of India and China, he also discovered that colonial exploitation, and opposition to it, were not limited to Africa.

The prison's debate program further helped to develop Malcolm's public speaking talent. He usually found a way to work the idea of race into his arguments, whether they were about military service or Shakespeare. Debate taught him rhetorical skills which he later used to earn converts to the Nation of Islam. He was thrilled by his success in making a white minister at the prison publicly admit that Jesus was not white. He resolved to devote the rest of his life to telling the white man about himself or to die trying.

Soon, Reginald, his brother, was suspended from the Nation of Islam for adultery and having a sexual affair with a secretary. After Master Fard appeared to Malcolm in a silent vision, Malcolm disowned Reginald and for the first time felt a stronger bond to his faith than to his family. Reginald went insane, and Malcolm came to believe that Allah was punishing Reginald for his sins. Malcolm continued to seek converts to the Nation of Islam among his fellow prisoners.

What was seldom recorded, however, centered on the teachings of Elijah Muhammad. I think more research should be done on the kinds of writers and scholars Elijah Muhammad read. We are sure that the religion of Islam, as defined by the late Honorable Elijah Muhammad, was influenced by the teachings of Master Fard, his predecessor, and that Elijah influenced the teachings and belief system of a young Malcolm. When we think of Malcolm being self-taught, we must not only include his time of imprisonment where he occupied himself in the reading of the many books at the library on the prison campus, but we must consider his sitting under the teachings of the Honorable Elijah Muhammad and formulating his own philosophy. We can assume that there were many teachings of the Quran and Holy Bible which were the basis of the many stories that both Malcolm and Elijah told.

Although Malcolm's non-formal education in his home was minimal because of his father's tragic death and his mother being taken out of the home after being deemed an unfit mother, during Malcolm's early life, his mother, being a very intelligent young woman and open to several religions, taught her son to embrace all religions. Although his mother was in the Christian faith with her husband who was an itinerant preacher going from one store front church to the other, she also accepted the faith of the Seventh Day Adventist Church and the religious statements of Garveyism.

When we think of the self-taught leader of one of the most powerful black movements of the 1960s, we must accept that Malcolm's earlier relationship with his father led him to both listen and hear the truth of the positive side of black history. After all, Marcus Garvey lifted up the black side of the Negro's rich history in Africa. Master Fard taught this to Elijah when moving into the Detroit neighborhood as both a voice and prophet bringing good news from the motherland of Africa.

As you grow up in the material universe, your world

view is shaped in subtle ways by your senses and your everyday experience. Your physical senses have a rather limited capacity. For example, science knows that there are many forms of light rays that your eyes cannot see. There is something beyond what your physical senses can detect, but the subtle message sent by your senses is that your options for changing your life are limited to the level of reality that can be detected by your senses.

Your senses also tell you that you live in a world that is primarily made up of a solid substance called "matter."

Your senses, furthermore, say that your physical body has very limited powers with changing matter. These powers can be extended through modern technology, but even technology sets strict boundaries for how much you can change your physical circumstances. Matter seems to be following laws that are largely beyond your control, and thus, there is only so much you can do to change the world of matter. According to your senses, your mind has no power to change your material circumstances.

As you grow up, you are surrounded by circumstances that seem to be beyond your control. You cannot change where you were born, your parents, or your society. You cannot change what neighborhood you were raised in and the influence it had on your mind and life. You cannot change your past and you, seemingly, have little, if any, influence on your future. The subtle message that is being programmed into your mind by your senses and everyday experience is that you are a limited being who has virtually no power to change your outer circumstances. This was not true for young Malcolm before his father's death and mother's forced imprisonment in an insane asylum.

Malcolm, I think, received a healthy dose of information about black people. On Sundays, his father would play the role of a traditional black preacher delivering historic sermons that are still being preached today. Malcolm had to have heard the stories of Moses and Pharaoh with the oppression of the Jewish nation and the miraculous crossing of the Red Sea. No doubt, Malcolm was there in church when he either heard his daddy preach or someone else tell the story of young David who defied Goliath and killed the giant with the swing of a sling and a stone. If his father was true to the black tradition of the Negro church in America, as E. Franklin Frazier calls it, then Malcolm was exposed to the religion of black folk in these traditional settings that led to the furthering of this self-taught leader of Americanized blacks.

What made this self-taught leader even more powerful

is that he undoubtedly understood the Christian side of black Americans and appreciated the Black side of the Negro. It is true that Malcolm's father, Earl, did go to the Negro church on Sundays, but during the week he was a proud follower of Marcus Garvey. Young Malcolm was born the same year Marcus Garvey was extradited to prison in Atlanta. However, his movement continued and remained both insightful and impactful during Malcolm's earlier life. Though there were few published works of African-Americans at the time, there were many who were able to perpetuate the oral tradition of Black people. We can assume through Garvey's schools that black education became a prime subject, and the lifting up of black heritage was a mandate of the school. It cannot be counted how many followers of Garvey remained steadfast to his United Negro Improvement Association (UNIA), but we can be sure that Earl Little was certainly one of them because he became a UNIA minister delivering the message during the week to those in his community. History bears the truth that Malcolm was his favorite son, and that father and son roamed the community sharing the message of the history and pride that came from being black in America.

Often Malcolm shared his love for the teaching of the Honorable Elijah Muhammad, but I think we can conclude that he was brilliant by the time he entered the eighth grade with his favorite English teacher, Mr. Ostrowski. Malcolm was so celebrated for his intelligence by his classmates that he was almost elected class president. The point being made is that even young Malcolm soaked up information, and no doubt retained it and could restate it.

Malcolm X, although self-taught, was highly educated. He learned much from the streets as a street hustler. He also learned much while in prison reading books from the library and staying up late, damaging his eyes because of a lack of light. His education expanded when he became an orthodox Muslim. Malcolm X transformed himself into a self-taught intellectual who spurned his past as a white-hating separatist and Nation of Islam advocate to become an orthodox Muslim and an international figure. As pointed out by many scholars, even though his transition was brief, it is apparent he became studious as a practicing orthodox Muslim. After his conversion to orthodox Islam and changing his name to El-Hajj Malik El-Shabazz in Mecca, he revised his vision of the movement and its leaders, might I remind you, through no formal education or training.

It was after April 13, 1964, that Malcolm X left the NOI and the United States on a personal and spiritual journey through the Middle East and West Africa. By the time he returned on May 21, he'd visited Egypt, Lebanon, Saudi Arabia, Nigeria, Ghana, Morocco and Algeria teaching himself so as to gain a better understanding of true Islam. Malcolm had changed again.

After first visiting Cairo, the Egyptian capital, Malcolm then visited Jeddah, Saudi Arabia, where he witnessed something he claimed he never saw in the United States: men of all colors and nationalities treating each other equally in the Islamic faith. "Throngs of people, obviously Muslims from everywhere, bound for the pilgrimage," he'd begun to notice at the airport terminal before boarding the plane for Cairo in Frankfurt, "were hugging and embracing." They were of all complexions, the whole atmosphere was of warmth and friendliness. The feeling hit me that there really wasn't any color problem here. The effect was as though I had just stepped out of a prison."

To enter the state of *ihram* required of all pilgrims heading for Mecca, Malcolm abandoned his trademark black suit and dark tie for the two-piece white garment pilgrims must drape over their upper and lower bodies. "Every one of the thousands at the airport, about to leave for Jeddah, was dressed this way," Malcolm wrote. "You could be a king or a peasant and no one would know."[2] That, of course, is the point of *ihram*. As Islam interprets it, it reflects the equality of man before God.

In Saudi Arabia, Malcolm had a second life-changing experience since leaving the Nation of Islam. As he fulfilled the Hajj, or pilgrimage to Mecca, he discovered an authentic Islamic faith of universal respect and brotherhood. Malcolm's world view was changed forever.

Finally, during the actual pilgrimage, he said, "My vocabulary cannot describe the new mosque that was being built around the Ka'aba." He described the sacred site as "a huge black stone house in the middle of the Great Mosque. It was being walked around by thousands upon thousands of praying pilgrims, both sexes, and every size, shape, color, and race in the world. My feeling here in the House of God was numbness. My *mutawaf* (religious guide) led me in the crowd of praying, chanting pilgrims, moving seven times around the Ka'aba. Some were bent with age; it was a sight that stamped itself on the brain."

It was that sight that inspired his famous "Letters from Abroad," three letters: one from Saudi Arabia, one from Nigeria, and one from Ghana. This sight began redefining Malcolm X's philosophy. "America," he wrote from Saudi Arabia on April 20, 1964, "needs to understand Islam, because this is the one religion that erases the race problem from its society."[3] He would later agree, "the white man is not inherently evil, but America's racist society influences him to act in an evil way." Malcolm changed and no longer accepted the teachings that whites were exclusively evil. Malcolm no longer called for black separatism. His pilgrimage to Mecca helped him discover the atoning power of Islam as a means to unity and self- respect. He wrote in Alex Haley's *The Autobiography of Malcolm X*, "In my thirty-nine years on this earth, the Holy City of Mecca had been the first time I had ever stood before the Creator of all and felt like a complete human being."

It had been a long journey in his brief life, but Malcolm had arrived to his final destination of total peace and correction of his separatist ideology and theology. It mostly occurred because Malcolm was not afraid to teach himself, and his self-teachings paid off.

---

1 Carson, Clayborne. Malcolm X: The FBI File (USA: Skyhorse Publishing, 2012), pg. 39.

2 Ibid., pg. 4

3 Ibid.

Chapter Five

ONE KING & HIS PALACES

THE KING OF SCLC

King was reared in the Ebenezer Baptist Church while Dexter Avenue Baptist Church in Montgomery served as his base church for the protests, therefore the church became his palace. In early January 1957, the leaders behind the Montgomery Bus Boycott assembled in Atlanta, Georgia, and founded the Southern Christian Leadership Conference, or SCLC. This became King's other palace. The SCLC, composed of churches and clergy from across the South, was created to coordinate protests inspired by the success of the bus boycott. The SCLC elected King as its president, for he had played a large part in its creation, and had, from the beginning, embodied the outlook and intellectual spirit of the group. He did much of the SCLC's fundraising by preaching and speaking in the North as well as in the South.

The SCLC was his newest palace. He became one man with two palaces: the church and the civil rights organization, the SCLC.

Although the SCLC was mostly a Christian organization, King had been encouraged by Bayard Rustin, an activist and communist sympathizer. Rustin helped with the effort in Montgomery and was one of a few non-clergy activists who affected and directed King's career. He, along with white Jewish radical, Stanley Levison, also of communist affiliations, and Ella Baker, a black social activist who worked extensively with the NAACP in the 1940s helped guide King's career by organizing events and writing letters, speeches, and books. King's association with Levison was strengthened early in 1957, but drew the attention of J. Edgar Hoover, director of the FBI under President Eisenhower. The FBI monitored and even harassed King, and at times, attempted to destroy his public campaigns and image through blackmail. It was alleged that King had sexual affairs, and the FBI's claim to know of them increased their capability to influence him. The FBI often attempted to dethrone King.

In February of 1957, the SCLC sent a message drafted by Levison and Rustin to then President Eisenhower, requesting that the White House hold a conference on civil rights. It was ignored by Eisenhower but caught the attention of the mass media. *TIME* magazine featured King on its cover, reinforcing the fame brought to him by the bus boycott. King's prominence also landed him an invitation, which he accepted, to celebrations of the independence of the African nation of Ghana from British colonial rule.

In May, King again made a national appearance, speaking at a rally of almost forty-thousand people in front of the Lincoln Memorial in Washington, D.C. The occasion marked the third anniversary of the *Brown v. Board of Education of Topeka, Kansas* ruling and examined its limited practical effects. Late in 1957, King launched, through the SCLC, the "Crusade for Citizenship," a program intended to help register two million black voters in time for the 1960 presidential election. The campaign was a failure for the SCLC because it did not include other civil rights organizations that would have helped in their success.

Other events in the life of Dr. King outside of the SCLC included the birth of his second child, Martin Luther King III, on October 23, 1957, and King's writing and publication of *Stride Toward Freedom* (1958), an account of the Montgomery Bus Boycott. The book sold well, and inspired other African-Americans to participate in the civil rights movement. King promoted the book during his speaking engagements, which continued. However, at a book signing in Harlem, he was stabbed by a mentally ill black woman, and survived only because the weapon, a letter opener, pierced him between his heart and one of his lungs. As part of his recovery time, King took a trip to India in February 1959, where he furthered his knowledge of nonviolent tactics at the Gandhi Peace Foundation.

When he returned from India, King committed himself more to the SCLC. He admitted that the Crusade for Citizenship had been a failure, and left his Dexter Avenue Baptist Church in Montgomery to move back to the SCLC headquarters in Atlanta, at the end of 1959. There, he resumed his position of assistant pastor under his father at Ebenezer Church, which freed him from the responsibilities of a full-time minister thus offering him more time to focus on the movement.

The move to Atlanta was an excellent decision as that winter there were spontaneous sit-in campaigns which began at whites-only lunch counters in Greensboro, North Carolina. These types of protests spread to scores of Southern cities. African-American college students, tired of segregated public facilities, protested with their peaceful presence. Tactics associated with King clearly inspired the campaign, and the SCLC became directly involved in April when Ella Baker helped organize the Student Nonviolent Coordinating Committee (SNCC) in Raleigh, North Carolina.

Later that year, King himself began to participate in sit-ins in an Atlanta department store, and there too, he was arrested. Despite his support and defense of the student actions, some of the protesters disassociated themselves from King, claiming that he was more talk than action. They charged him with taking credit for the money and fame that others earned through sacrifice. This impression only deepened when King, through the help of presidential candidate, John F. Kennedy, left the Atlanta jail early. According to the more aggressive members of SNCC, one's time in jail measured one's devotion to the cause. Kennedy's willingness to help King was due to his rather mainstream appeal. Kennedy needed the votes of white Southerners, and many blacks now felt that if King could appeal to these white voters, he was not truly representing them.

Many suggest that King too readily compromised with whites. It was sometimes said that he used his prominence to exempt himself from the tests of dedication. This assertion followed him throughout his career. King, however, seemed always to consider how he could best serve the movement, and rightly believed that he could be most effective out of jail. King attracted further criticism for what, by this time, was his strict adherence to principles of absolute pacifism, a course not accepted by some members of the Student Nonviolent Coordinating Committee, despite the name of their organization. Some of them felt there were times when a violent response was necessary.

In the summer of 1961, King started working with the Freedom Riders, a campaign of bus trips from north to south, intended to desegregate bus stations and lunch counters. They gladly used volunteers from the North. The Congress of Racial Equality, or CORE, had organized the Freedom Rides without King's help, and King limited his involvement to training participants in methods of nonviolence, and to negotiating with the Kennedy administration.

Those who participated in these Freedom Riders were met with violence. Sometimes the tires on their cars were slashed, their buses burned, their persons attacked, and King questioned whether the gains were worth the losses. When he declined to participate in one of the Freedom Rides, his commitment was questioned.

Within less than a year, John F. Kennedy's handling of

civil rights issues was disappointing to King and other civil rights leaders. Kennedy depended on Southern Democrats, and had even appointed some segregationists to judgeships in the South. Robert Kennedy, the attorney general and brother of the president, was an ally of King, but not without condition. He was foremost his brother's brother. He shared his brother's political allegiances to certain Southerners, and was apprehensive to police the South through law enforcement agencies. At King's suggestion, he did intervene to protect the Freedom Riders. The Attorney General ordered the Interstate Commerce Commission, or ICC, to ban segregation in interstate travel, thus giving official federal support to the Freedom Rides. This, King appreciated.

Consequently, the Freedom Rides were CORE's program, not King's, and late in 1961, King turned his attention to the plight of racism in Albany, Georgia. With the Albany Movement, as it became known, King attached himself to a protest already in progress. He did this with the Freedom Riders in Montgomery as well. SNCC had already established a voter-registration center in the heavily segregated city, and this, in turn, had provided a base of operations for various sit-ins and protests in Albany's public places. King stepped in when he felt the movement could not afford to give up any more of its members to the prisons and jails.

Martin arrived on December 15, 1961, with Ralph Abernathy and led a march of protesters to City Hall. All the protesters were arrested. However, Albany Police Chief Laurie Pritchett handled his prisoners very courteously which diffused and watered down the effects of King's nonviolent protest. Pritchett had studied King's method of nonviolence and understood that with no physical conflict there was no media blitz and no national outrage. Nevertheless, negotiations followed the mass arrests and appeared to be little victory for the protesters. King, who had vowed to remain in jail until demands were met, left when City authorities made several verbal and written promises. But appearances were deceiving. For example, the city of Albany promised to desegregate bus and rail terminals as if in response to the protests, even though statutes already required it to do so. The city did not submit to further promises of desegregation by shutting down the public institutions in question.

What King and Abernathy did next was to return to Albany in February to get ready for the December rally. While they had been away, the media had left too, and the city had refused to negotiate with the SNCC protesters who remained. King and Abernathy were sentenced to jail in July, but returning again revived the interest of the media. King and Abernathy refused to pay the fine that would have exempted them from serving time, but local authorities, sensing the publicity of their incarceration decided to pay the fine for them instead of keeping them in jail.

While King and Abernathy were still in Albany, young protesters, who had been fighting nonviolently for months, were becoming impatient and frustrated and thus turned to violence. A crowd of two thousand threw rocks and bottles at police. King tried to stop the violence, and held a prayer vigil against it, but was arrested for this. Again, he was kept from being jailed, and, soon after, the city obtained a federal injunction banning King and his followers from protesting. Until this point, King had fought local laws on the grounds of the federal laws to fight against local laws. In this case, protest would mean violation of what King claimed was his legal foundations.

Police Chief Pritchett's gentle methods of dealing with the protesters and the City's refusal to jail King, along with the pressure from Robert Kennedy who encouraged King to continue to abide by federal laws created a slim chance for victory in Albany. King left the city in August in failure, having learned what not to do. In his next campaign in Birmingham, Alabama, he would avoid these mistakes and watch for the pitfalls.

In May 1962, Birmingham minister and SCLC member, Rev. Fred Shuttlesworth, suggested that the SCLC join with his own organization, the Alabama Christian Movement for Human Rights, to protest segregated conditions in Birmingham. Birmingham was the wealthiest city in Alabama, and mostly segregated. The mayor was a segregationist and the Commissioner of Public Safety, Eugene "Bull" Conner, was as well. He was known for his hostile and sometimes violent treatment of blacks. The governor of the state was George Wallace, who had won office with promises of "segregation now, segregation tomorrow, segregation forever."

In Birmingham, between 1957 and 1962, seventeen black churches and homes were bombed, including the home of Rev. Shuttlesworth, who campaigned actively for civil rights. Although the population of Birmingham was nearly half black, there seemed little hope for a political solution to the racial divide: of the majority registered voters, only about ten percent were black.

King decided not to embrace Rev. Shuttlesworth's suggestion until early 1963. Once he did, he treated it as a major campaign. In March, King, along with Ralph Abernathy and a few other SCLC organizers, set up headquarters in a room at a motel in one of Birmingham's black neighborhoods. They began recruiting volunteers for protest rallies and giving workshops in nonviolent techniques. Initially, King scheduled the protests to begin in time to disrupt the Easter shopping season, giving them economic advantage. However, he postponed his plans to prevent them from affecting the local mayoral election, in which Bull Conner was a candidate.

The Birmingham campaign began on April 3rd with lunch-counter sit-ins. On April 6th, protesters marched on City Hall, and forty-two people were arrested. Demonstrations occurred each day thereafter. While the jails filled up with peaceful blacks, King negotiated with white businessmen, whose stores were losing business due to the protests. Although some of these businessmen were willing to consider desegregating their facilities and hiring blacks, city officials held fast to segregationist policies. On April 10th, these officials obtained an injunction prohibiting the demonstrations. Unlike the injunction in Albany, Georgia, however, this one came from a state court, not a federal one. King felt comfortable violating such an injunction, on the grounds of adhering to the federal laws with which it was at odds.

King finally got the other leaders of the campaign to violate the injunction, however, it took some real convincing by King, especially since many of the clergy felt obligated to be in their churches on Easter with as many congregants as possible, and not in jail. King successfully persuaded them to join him in his cause, and personally led the march on Good Friday, April 12th. All protesters were quickly arrested. Birmingham police separated King and Abernathy, placing them in solitary confinement, and denying them their rightful phone calls to the outside world.

Coretta, King's wife, was disturbed by the unprecedented silence from her husband and she called the White House. Her call was returned by Robert Kennedy and then by the president himself. The Kennedy administration sent FBI agents to Birmingham, and King received kinder treatment. Moreover, this intervention by Kennedy gave the movement greater momentum.

King spent eight days in his cell. During that time, he composed one of the most powerful letters of his career, "Letter from a Birmingham Jail." The letter was created in response to a letter by white members of the clergy that was recently run in a local newspaper, which claimed that the protests were "unwise, untimely, and uninvited." King quite deliberately wrote his letter of response for not only the local clerics, but to the entire nation. The letter revealed King's strength as a speaker and his vast education from institutions of higher learning. It contained in it many secular thoughts, as well as Biblical parallels. It was most passionate and subsequently appropriated by many writing textbooks as a model of persuasive writing and language. At the time, it gave a singular, eloquent voice to a massive movement. The letter from the Birmingham Jail established him further as the king who could not only speak from the steps of Washington, but also from a jail cell in Birmingham. The king of civil rights had effectively again risen to his height in the depth of a jail cell. He wrote more like the Apostle Paul incarcerated in a Philippian jail cell writing one of the greatest epistles the world has ever known.

Chapter Six

THE INTEGRATIONIST KING

IS RELEASED

Once King was released from jail, the protests assumed a larger scale and a more confrontational character. At the suggestion of SCLC representative, Rev. Jim Bevel, the organizers began to recruit younger protesters. They visited high schools, training youth in nonviolent tactics. The method was dangerous. They understood that those kids could get hurt. Furthermore, potentially and very symbolically powerful, King understood that children were the beneficiaries of the movement. The children and youth represented the movement's hope for the future.

On May 2, 1963, King addressed a young crowd at the Sixteenth Street Baptist Church. Afterward, they marched downtown, singing "We Shall Overcome," and nearly a thousand youth showed up and were arrested. The next day, younger people had arrived to replenish the ranks, and another march occurred. By this time, the situation had become overwhelming for Bull Conner, whose jails were full. On May 3, he had his police officers and firefighters blast the young protesters with powerful water force from fire-hoses, as well as release attack dogs against them. It was these acts of violence broadcast on national television that pricked the national conscience, and marked a turning point not only in Birmingham, but also in the Civil Rights Movement as a whole. Telegrams and calls flooded the White House conveying outrage, and it became clear that the Kennedy administration would have to confront civil rights issues more directly in America.

Very soon, the protests became so massive and volatile that the city was willing to negotiate. It listened to the demands of the SCLC and set a schedule for the desegregation of lunch counters and other facilities. It also promised to confront the issue of inequality in hiring practices, to release the arrested demonstrators, and to create a biracial committee to settle their differences.

Consequently, the same thing that happened in Montgomery soon happened in Birmingham. Violence followed the agreement. Whites bombed black homes and churches, and blacks retaliated with mob violence. King's activities in Birmingham, therefore, included a final stage, during which he patrolled the city, speaking wherever people had gathered and imploring blacks to answer violence with peaceful means.

While changes in local policies constituted the Birmingham campaign's immediate outcome, the effort's long-term effects were felt across the nation. In the weeks that followed, tensions flared, and protests began again in numerous Southern cities. On June 11, President Kennedy voiced his commitment to federal civil rights legislation. He had been holding off, but Birmingham pressed the issue. Kennedy's commitment culminated in the passing of the Civil Rights Act of 1964, which was signed into law by Lyndon Johnson after Kennedy's assassination. The act mandated federally what had in Birmingham been won locally: a white commitment to desegregation and equal employment opportunities.

On August 28, 1963, roughly 250,000 people, three quarters of them black, marched in Washington, D.C., from the Washington Monument to the Lincoln Memorial, where they listened to speeches by America's civil rights leaders, including King. Officially called the "March on Washington for Jobs and Freedom," the event was a major success as the preceding Birmingham campaign had been and, like that campaign, contributed to the atmosphere in which federal civil rights legislation could pass.

The planning of the rally had been a group effort, involving A. Phillip Randolph, Martin Luther King, Jr., James Farmer of CORE, Roy Wilkins of the NAACP, John Lewis of SNCC, and Dorothy Height of the National Council of Negro Women. Bayard Rustin became its national coordinator. The plan initially upset the Kennedy administration, which feared riots would result, and thus endanger the civil rights legislation that had recently come before Congress. Consequently, the administration became involved in the planning, editing the content of each of the speakers speeches, inviting white organizations to participate, and thereby, successfully preventing the outbreak of violence. This involvement led militant blacks to consider the march an inauthentic event such as the Nation of Islam representative, Malcolm X, who dismissed it altogether, although he attended the march as an outside critic.[1]

The attendees of the march exceeded the expectations of its planners: they had counted on 100,000 and got a quarter of a million. At the rally, King was the last speaker to address the marchers, and he delivered the most famous speech of his career. The speech titled, "I Have a Dream," was passionate, rhythmic, and clear as King described his hopes for the future.

The speech aired on national television, reaching millions

of Americans, including President Kennedy, who watched from the White House. It aided the Civil Rights Movement by providing a clear articulation of the hopes and wishes behind their actions that often seemed confusing. Even on television, King was a speaker with tremendous presence.

The joy of the Birmingham and Washington victories was offset by murders throughout the South. In Mississippi on May 12, Medgar Evers, a friend of King and an active NAACP member, was shot dead at the door to his home. On September 15, at the Sixteenth Street Baptist Church in Birmingham, from which King had led marches during the spring campaign, four little black girls died when a bomb exploded. On November 22, John F. Kennedy was assassinated in Dallas, Texas. These tragedies counterbalanced all the civil rights movement's victories.[2]

Nevertheless, more victories came. In January 1964, King appeared again on the cover of *TIME* Magazine, this time as the magazine's "Man of the Year." During the summer, King spoke in East and West Germany and met with the Pope. He also campaigned for Johnson's reelection, against Johnson's very conservative Republican opponent, Barry Goldwater. In July, Johnson invited King to the White House when he signed into law the Civil Rights Act of 1964, which King helped to precipitate with the Birmingham campaign. The meeting reassured King of Johnson's priorities.

King's SCLC activities that year took him to St. Augustine, Florida, early in the summer. There, protesters attempting to integrate the town were suffering the violence of the Ku Klux Klan. Four people had died in bombings, and the Klan was organizing mobs to attack civil rights workers when they came to segregated sites. King, Abernathy, and others were arrested for attempting to eat at a whites-only restaurant, but King left jail early to receive an honorary doctoral degree from Yale University. His absence hurt the campaign in St. Augustine. An injunction was soon passed banning marches, and the federal government refused to intervene. The city then became the site of another of SCLC's failures.[3]

Also filled with violence and mixed results was that summer's voter registration campaign in Mississippi, known as "Freedom Summer." "Freedom Summer" involved cooperation between SCLC, SNCC, CORE, and the NAACP, which together pushed to register as many blacks as possible. The murder of three civil rights workers, under suspicious circumstances involving local police, created problems for the campaign. When King initiated a march to protest the atmosphere of hostility and violence, the police halted the event with tear gas and rifles.

King's fame reached its peak in October of that year, when he was informed that he had won the Nobel Peace Prize for 1964. On December 10, the Nobel Committee honored him at a ceremony in Oslo, Norway. King announced that he accepted the honor on behalf of the Civil Rights Movement, to which he would give all $54,000 of the prize money to the several civil rights organizations. However, by early 1965, the Nobel Prize Laureate was back in a jail cell in the southern United States. The SCLC organization was working and protesting again and so was Martin.

The released King was captured by a new idea and mission after 1965. Between 1965 and 1968, Dr. King shifted his focus toward economic justice which he highlighted by leading several campaigns in Chicago. His idea for international peace became apparent when he began championing opposition to the Vietnam War. His work in these years culminated in the "Poor People's Campaign," which was a broad effort to assemble a multiracial coalition of impoverished Americans who would advocate for economic change.

The released King was a different kind of king because his target was not just social and political integration. Dr. King was now about to confront the American system in a much different way and at an unprecedented level. At that time, America still believed in strong patriotism by its citizens and talk against the government's involvement in the Vietnam War was unacceptable by mainstream black and white leaders. No peace-loving American at the time would have gone against the government, the president, and the nation as King did after 1965. King understood that the two laws he needed most passed, the Civil Rights Act and Voting Rights Act had been signed, sealed, and delivered to the nation. Consequently, with their passage, King could move on to other campaigns. King went after the unjust war in Vietnam.

The immediate attack on the war in Vietnam was looked upon by President Lyndon B. Johnson as an attack on a so-called friend and ally of the civil rights movement. After all, it was Johnson who passed these bills during his administration and did so in hopes that King would never challenge the president on the war in Vietnam. Few knew the real economic cost of the war and with Johnson's escalation of the war so increased the cost. The true cost of continuing the war was hidden, and only the eyes of a few within Johnson's administration knew what the real cost had been.

King's problem occurred when he gave his antiwar speech at Riverside Church on April 4, 1967, before a huge crowd of some of the most influential people in America including John D. Rockefeller, and a host of media representatives from across the world. King's speech, "Time to Break the Silence," was not only oratorically beautiful with the tones, expressions, and intensity of an orator of the highest of caliber, but it was accurate in substance and on target as to the kind of information he was giving. The war had been too costly. Too many American lives had been taken and a high casualty rate per population of African-Americans was unfair and those men and women returning to a community of poverty was even more unwarranted.

King connected two major ideas that would lead to his death exactly one year to the date: the war in Vietnam and the war on poverty both were too costly for America. As King eloquently stated, "America cannot fight two wars at the same time: A War on Poverty and a War in Vietnam." His understanding of how these two promotions in America would lead to disastrous ends for the nation became too much for the Johnson's administration to bear. This led not only to a different kind of King, but to a president's additional list of perplexing problems, causing Johnson to refuse to accept his nomination as the president for another term at the next Democratic convention. Johnson retired.

Though the King who was released from the Birmingham jail regained his momentum after being incarcerated as a criminal, King was never the same after 1965. King suddenly experienced health issues not seen before in the past. During the earlier protests, King was known to have checked himself in the hospital as his way of getting a few days of rest. King maintained an extremely busy schedule seldom seeing his wife and children throughout the year. He was in constant route from city to city, church to church, street to street, until he found himself at the point of total exhaustion. King was also getting older. He was not the twenty-six-year-old King of Montgomery, but he was nearing his forties which he would never see.

Many of his friends began noticing his rapidly aging face, his complaining of stomach problems, and the painful look of depression and worry on his face. King was now getting tired. Andrew Young explained in the years after King's death how he noticed Martin was not as jovial as in the past. Although it is true that on the night of his death, King and his assistants, Ralph and Andrew, were involved in a childish pillow fight in the hotel room they stayed in in Memphis. However, Young also shared how this became one of the fewer fun moments; they were having a relaxing moment because King was not merely tired but exhausted.

Many began not only distancing themselves from King due to his opposition of the Vietnam War and the threat of pulling financial support from all the civil rights organizations by governmental officials, but some were concerned of the allegations of his numerous infidelities. Perhaps, King's bouts with depression and over exhaustion may have led to his not putting his vulnerabilities in check. Only he and those whom he may have been involved with know for sure. What we do know is that other than a few questionable tapes of King's alleged affairs by J. Edgar Hoover and the FBI, King may have well been exonerated from even these allegations. We must remember that what we read and hear regarding these fleeting moments of adultery are usually one-sided by those who claimed to have been with King. Never have we the assurance that King directly admitted to these affairs. It is true that when King was questioned about the affairs by those who believed the FBI had something on him, he only admits "they may have something," but does not say exactly what those things may have been. Furthermore, we cannot altogether trust the reports of the FBI which was doing its best to take King down.

The released King of 1963 becomes the broken King after 1965. People from every spectrum of life began distancing themselves from him. Friends moved away from him like he had a plague. His own wife, Coretta, even questioned his loyalty to marriage and on occasions thought to divorce him, but did not do so because of the advice and influence of others. It was indeed encouraging to know that Jacquelyn Kennedy, JFK's wife, helped her to understand what it meant to be married to a national leader like King and to hear of the innuendos regarding her husband. After all, JFK was accused of having several affairs with the famous performer, Marilyn Monroe, as well as, other former girlfriends. These all added to the pressures of Martin who just years earlier was on the front page of *TIME* as the "Man of the Year," now being shunned by not only the press but his closest friend. Sometimes, in such a situation it is better to have a kid's pillow fight than to continue a course that would lead to suicide.

It is true, according to people like Andrew Young who reflected on the life of MLK, that he felt that King was possibly suicidal. Young reported on numerous television programs after King's death that Martin may have had a martyr complex, and that not only did Martin know, but they knew that death was inevitable. They all were just awaiting the moment. Often time, King talked about who would speak and what would be said at his funeral. Sometimes he would be serious as in the speech played at his funeral at Ebenezer Baptist Church; other times they joked about it as they did the evening of his death.

I would conclude here that the physically released King of 1963 became the spiritually released King of 1968 at Mason Temple in Memphis, Tennessee, where he gives his last prophetic speech. What outside observers failed to realize was that when a man like King is on stage, it is the pulpit where he acts out his pain and frustrations, and where he can feel the exuberant experience of his total life. When a preacher is giving what King was taught by his earlier professor, Dr. George Kelsey, Sociologist professor at Morehouse, a sermon which is both drama and theology acted out on the stage of the pulpit can be most releasing of one's burden and spirituality. When King stood at Mason Temple declaring I've Been to the Mountaintop, he was not only making a declaration, but he was experiencing a personal release and a kind of interaction not only between him and the congregational audience, but between him and God. O my, what a release it was! Not only did nearly 3,000 people jump, shout, and cry, but the world taped the last sermon and to this day people continue to hear it with joy.

1 Cone, James. H. *Martin & Malcolm & America: A Dream or a Nightmare.* Maryknoll, NY: Orbis Books, 1991, pg. 2

2 Ibid., pg. 86

3 Ibid.

Chapter Seven
THE NATIONALIST KING
IS RELEASED

Malcolm Little goes into prison as a pimp, a drug addict, and a man of violence, but comes out looking like a minister. The prison released Malcolm in August 1952 and placed him on parole in the care of his brother, Wilfred. Malcolm had been transformed by the prison, rehabilitated from his criminal ways, and ready to move into Nationalism. He was released not only physically, but mentally and spiritually.

He had a new attitude expressed by three things: A wristwatch, a suitcase and a pair of eyeglasses. Malcolm bought a wristwatch, a suitcase, and a pair of eyeglasses to symbolize the new Malcolm. He was headed for kingship and leadership in the Nation of Islam organization. The wristwatch, suitcase, and eyeglasses each symbolized an important aspect of Malcolm's new career as a Muslim minister, a political figure, and a leader. The wristwatch represented his preoccupation with managing his time rightfully and keeping up with a busy daily schedule.

He was committed to the people and movements of his daily life. He planned to stay close to the Honorable Elijah Muhammad and other Muslim religious leaders. The suitcase represented Malcolm's commitment to a life of constant work and frequent travel taking care of business in the name of spreading Islam. He was doing business for the Nation as a businessperson. His travels allowed him to interact with other blacks nationwide and other minorities worldwide, and such experiences helped him develop a more mature perspective on the struggle of black people against oppression. Malcolm's eyeglasses represented his newfound clarity of vision on race in America. Though the glasses serve the practical purpose of correcting his vision problems Malcolm developed from years of reading in prison, they also serve the symbolic purpose of correcting his understanding of the issues at hand. He said, "In all my years in the streets, I'd been looking at the exploitation that for the first time I really saw and understood." This shows that his time in prison made him see the race problem clearly. With his commitment to his message, his connection to his people, and understanding of the problems plaguing his people, Malcolm was prepared to push himself into a new and productive life.

Malcolm instantly appreciated the order of Wilfred's strictly Muslim household. The solidarity and sternness of his strict adherence to Nation of Islam temple meetings created a sense of excitement in Malcolm. In Chicago, Elijah Muhammad publicly likened Malcolm to the biblical figure Job, inviting everyone to watch the strength of Malcolm's faith now that the hedge of the prison bars were gone and he was back out among the temptations of the real world. Malcolm inquired of Elijah Muhammad about recruitment techniques and strategies as he was eager to work to attract and disciple new members in Detroit. Elijah Muhammad advised Malcolm to appeal to young people and make them his newest converts. Elijah is no doubt aware of the vulnerability and openness to new thoughts and ideas.

In Detroit, Malcolm has little luck at first persuading only a few neighborhood youth to visit the temple. Over several months, however, membership tripled. During this period, Malcolm replaced his last name with "X"to represent the unknown African name he would have had if his ancestors had not been kidnapped and enslaved. Malcolm began to speak at temple meetings and gains confidence from his listeners as a great speaker. He is surprised, humbled, and flattered when Elijah Muhammad appointed him as the assistant minister at the Detroit temple.

It was not long before Malcolm learned not only the religion of the Nation of Islam, but the background of Elijah Muhammad's life story. Elijah was born in Georgia in 1897. Though Elijah Muhammad was small of stature, Malcolm soon learned how bold and tall this man could be in vision, character, and insight, especially when it came to issues of race. Malcolm learned Elijah moved to Detroit. In 1931, Elijah Muhammad met Wallace D. Fard, who sold coats, fine silk, and trinkets and became the self proclaimed prophet who converted him to his version of Islam. By the time Fard disappeared in 1934, Elijah Muhammad was one of the major leaders of the Nation of Islam. Death threats from jealous members of the sect compelled Elijah Muhammad to move himself and his family from city to city for seven years for safety sake. Supposedly, he spent time in prison for draft evasion, although he was too old to serve in the military. Only in the 1940s did he reclaim his position as the rightful head of the Nation of Islam.

Malcolm X became the right kind of person to grow the NOI. Soon the sect grew from a mere 400 active membership to over 100,000 or possibly 200,000 committed followers by 1960. Malcolm X quit his job at the Ford Motor Company and began extensive and intensive training for followers holding massive membership drives. During this time, he fully developed his oratorical style. When Malcolm was ready, Elijah Muhammad sent him to Boston to help in the creation of a temple there. Malcolm visited old familiar territory and tried to convert his old prison friend Shorty, who told Malcolm how much he still loved white women, pork, and the street hustling community to be converted to any religion. However, Ella, his half sister was amazed at Malcolm's change, and although she did not convert to Islam herself, she was happy to see that he was transformed in a positive way, and she became extremely supportive of Malcolm's practice of his new faith.

Soon, Malcolm had the Boston temple up and running. Elijah Muhammad sent Malcolm to Philadelphia. Early in the summer of 1954, Muhammad appointed Malcolm to organize the small New York Temple. In Boston, Malcolm sought out his old crowd. He discovered that Sammy the Pimp whom he associated with before prison life was dead and that West Indian Archie was dying. Malcolm became somewhat disappointed in his lack of recruitment ability. The lack of response to his initial teachings frustrated Malcolm, but he continued on and the temple in Boston soon grew. Malcolm and his followers developed a strategy for drawing blacks from other Black Nationalist rallies that advocated a return to Africa. He also stood on the outside of churches appealing to weak Christians to return to the religion of their motherland, Islam. Malcolm had so much luck winning over Christians that he changed his speaking style and message with them in mind. He emphasized Christianity's role in the oppression of blacks from historical, biblical, and theological perspectives.

By the time 1956 came around, Malcolm was not only popular with the male part of the nation, but the female counterpart and a particular female member he found himself attracted to. Her name is Betty Dean Sanders who joined the New York temple. Initially, Betty was a registered nurse. For ten years, Malcolm had vowed celibacy and was fully devoted to his work. He hardly courted Betty, but he approved of her from a distance. Malcolm introduced Betty to Elijah Muhammad, and then he proposed marriage from a pay phone in Detroit. She accepted, and after they married and move to Queens, New York, four children were born while Malcolm was alive and a fifth child was born after Malcolm's death.

In 1958, Malcolm's half-sister, Ella, converted to the Nation of Islam. The Nation became prominent when police attacked one of its members. The "Fruit of Islam," the Nation's elite youth male group, led a mass demonstration, standing quietly before the police precinct house where the bleeding victim was being held and not given proper hospital assistance. Malcolm and the men stood in front of the hospital until they heard from a doctor as to the status of the member's health. Later, the Nation of Islam won a large sum of money in a lawsuit against the city. Malcolm was so busy that the Nation finally bought him a car to use for his travel between cities. Having taken a vow of poverty, Malcolm had access to the Nation's substantial resources, but personally owned almost nothing and took home only a little more than nothing monetarily. By 1965, there were large temples in Chicago, Detroit, and New York.

The problem was that Malcolm had the right method for attracting members and he thought he had the right message. It was only until he split from the nation in 1964 that he learned he had been teaching a perverted message of Islam. He was not aware of this until after the ninety day silence by Elijah for speaking out against the death of President John F. Kennedy.

Scholars for years lifted Malcolm up as a savior to the black masses. He was a kind of "king" to the oppressed. It is true that Malcolm challenged black people in America to both learn and appreciate their culture and history being descendants of Africans. He understood the long years of toll that Americanized slavery had taken on the lives of black people. He was an excellent self-taught historian who understood the residuals of slavery on the thoughts and actions of the people of the oppressed. He was well aware of the black and white struggle that affected everything from where a person could live, sleep, be healed, and even be employed.

Perhaps, Malcolm was one of the best persons to analyze segregation and integration in American society at the time. Malcolm needed more than a solely self-reliance perspective and program for black people. The wristwatch, suitcase, and eyeglasses were not enough for him to see the total solution to racism and discrimination and certainly the slanted teachings of the Honorable Elijah Muhammad. Malcolm himself admitted this, having to split from the NOI organization and informed the world that Elijah was wrong!

In the Nation, Malcolm X was persuaded to believe in an incomplete mixture of blackness, socialism, and self-imposed erroneous teaching of Islam. Malcolm admitted this when he converted to orthodox Islam. Though he had been released from prison, he now became a prisoner of Elijah Muhammad's negative solutions to the problems of America and, in particular, black Americans. Not even a new pair of eyeglasses could help him to see the errors of the ways of Elijah Muhammad. It is true,

Malcolm took no credit for applauding the death of President John F. Kennedy, but the truth of the matter is Malcolm's expressions and lack of sympathy for his family and children in their sudden loss is a clear indicator that he did not know the true Islamic faith statements. Had he known he would have been much more careful with his slip of the tongue, "the chickens have come home to roost," to which the media interpreted, as well as many others as being insensitive and glad over the death of the president. At the very least, when people and families have experienced this kind of loss there ought to be a tone of empathy, after all, the Kennedy children lost their father suddenly through death. He, too, became fatherless without notice and felt the pains of personal death and should have been more empathetic at this personal moment for the family and this national moment for the country. After all, like he assumed his father was murdered, John F. Kennedy was publicly assassinated.

As we look at Malcolm's teaching on blackness based upon what the Honorable Elijah Muhammad taught, we will quickly see flaws in his lessons. Although African-Americans came from Africa and had been here in America for over 244 years of legalized slavery and 100 years of segregation, they had made some progress towards integration. You cannot say merely because there are some deniable rights that you have not made some progress. Reconstruction period at the very least relieved the slaves from the mandates of the plantations Segregation certainly was better than slavery. The sole solution for equality as Martin pointed out, was not to leave America to go back to another nation, like Africa. After all, you have a vested interest in America. Also, a feasibility study would have told the Nation they had not a solid plan to return to Africa. They had no ships or resources to export eleven million blacks to Africa. Also, to take claim of five fertile states in America as Malcolm recommended did not include a governmental arrangement by both Christians and non-Christian movements such as the Nation. Who will govern the new nation and under what religion and constitution? We see how that lack of agreement is playing out all over Africa today in intertribal and intranational wars and killings.

The truth of the matter is, both Marcus Garvey and Malcolm X were wrong to teach that when citizenship is not given rightful inheritance, then you remove yourself and go back to Africa especially in the then context of America. Africa may be for the Africans but not for invested African-Americans. Perhaps, that is what we can appreciate about Martin Luther King, Jr.; he had an "American Dream" and not a "Black" or "White" Dream, but a dream that included all Americans.

Malcolm's method and message of blackness was most enlightening but not ultimately liberating. It certainly was a misfire from reality. When you look at King's method of going to the March on Washington, at the very least, he ends up getting the passage of two very important pieces of national legislation: the Civil Rights Act and Voting Bill. When you hear the tone and tenure of Malcolm X in New York City, there is frustration in his voice, anger on his face, and dissatisfaction within his organization. However, anger does not always produce very much when America's ruling class is not willing to cooperate with you. King understood that Malcolm's approach would only alienate whites.[1]

What we learn about Malcolm is that his street-like thuggish ways were carried over into his politics. America is a democracy, and it would, then and now, be hard to force America into submitting to a blackmail kind of posture. To go to the South while King is in jail and publicly release a statement to his wife, Coretta, suggesting that those in white America ought to speak and negotiate with the kinder and gentler King would be advisable or they will have an angry Malcolm X to deal with is totally thuggish. Perhaps, had he sat with the unity of all Black Nationalist and Negro Integrationist organization to submit to a certain posture would have been more effective, but I do not think it would have been more plausible. America may have listened, and such thoughts and statements would have been far more appropriate and helpful. Malcolm soon learned that threats of violence could ultimately lead to a life of crime and a following of angry uncontrollable black men who would end up getting you killed.

Certainly, we cannot say that everything Malcolm taught was thuggish. We must give him credit for leading his followers in the ritualistic life of a true Islamic follower. Teaching prayer and reading of the Quran is helpful for a true believer in that religion. Leading people to levels of responsibility for their family members is honorable. Controlling one's food diet is needful for good health. However, to teach "An eye for eye and life for a life"is not always the suitable way to win battles. In many cases, it will, as King noted, get both you and the offender blind sighted. I think America has learned that recently with the problems we've had in getting in the War in Iraq that it is better not to always respond with a hothead reaction to a problem. Sometimes it's better in the human family to exercise patience, wisdom, and love as Martin Luther King attempted to show.

I do not think during the latter part of Malcolm's life that he was internally released and at peace with himself. He constantly heard of the infidelity rumors of his leader, the Honorable Elijah Muhammad. One of the young women that Elijah is accused of birthing a baby by was one of the members of the Nation of Islam whom Malcolm had personal affection for and possibly would have married had he not been married to Betty. Of course, that's an assertion.

No, Malcolm was not at peace with himself, especially when Betty, his wife, continued to challenge him for what he was being financially reimbursed for his service to the Nation. His compensation package included a car and moderate size house and some pocket change, while Elijah held the key to the Nation's safe. We must also remember neither Malcolm nor King had adequate life or death insurance, and Malcolm needed a collection plate to even provide for his final funeral and burial services that was held outside of the NOI organization and in a Pentecostal church.

The question becomes, how can a man be at peace and not able to adequately provide for his family even when he makes a personal vow of poverty? The complications of struggling with money issues caused the integrity of your leader to be in question and then wondering if the whole ideology of the Nation is truth gives Malcolm much to ponder. Being castigated by the NOI and being a leader who was being silenced for what Malcolm calls a mere slip of the tongue had to create internal turmoil for Malcolm. No, Malcolm was not at peace especially learning that members of his organization were out to kill him sanctioned by a short blurb in the NOI newspaper to which Louis Farrakhan suggested that such a man as Malcolm was worthy of death for his non-allegiance to the Honorable Elijah Muhammad. Malcolm finally broke from the nation.

Taking the hajj or pilgrimage to Mecca was helpful to Malcolm's sense of peace. He discovered that orthodox Islamic taught unity of humanity regardless of one's skin color. He soon allowed the racial or black god to die in a mortal battle with a nonracial god in the true orthodox Islamic faith. His ideology changed, but he had not the time nor academic luxury to work it out in his mind. His life would be cut short in less than a year. He was a black leader, and although he shifted his organization, Organization of African-American Unity, to different aims, he struggled with the identity of Malcolm X and El- Hajj Malik El-Shabazz internally. He answered to the news media as soon as he landed back in America after taking his pilgrimage, as to whether or not he will still be known as "Malcolm X."He responded by saying as long as the struggles of blacks in America remain, there was still a need for a Malcolm X. Malcolm was not sure as to what form the new Malcolm X would take in his message to the people. He was still somewhat confused. However, we cannot be sure we will ever understand how clear Malcolm was on his newfound religion because his life was soon taken away in death. Perhaps, death became the ultimate release and peace that Malcolm needed from his struggles of identity.

It was on the evening of February 21, 1965, at the Audubon Ballroom in Manhattan, where Malcolm X was about to deliver a speech, three assassins rushed to the stage and shot him 15 times at close range. Malcolm X was pronounced dead on arrival at Columbia Presbyterian Hospital shortly thereafter. He was 39 years old. The three men convicted of the assassination of Malcolm X were all members of the Nation of Islam: Talmadge Hayer, Norman 3X Butler, and Thomas 15X Johnson.

In the immediate aftermath of Malcolm X's death, scholars seldom understood and interpreted his spiritual and political transformation into the Orthodox Islamic faith and criticized him as being merely a violent rabble-rouser. Malcolm was dead! This gave Martin Luther King a greater platform from which to continue pushing his nonviolent campaign. When asked for a response to the death of Malcolm, King said very little.

However, even though Malcolm X's legacy continued, it does so in a limited fashion. He was ousted and excommunicated by the Nation, and hardly understood by those attempting to understand him in his last phase of existence. He was seen as a civil rights hero. And although his life, works, and words are written in the 1965 publication of *The Autobiography of Malcolm X: As Told by Alex Haley*, which excited many at the time, Malcolm still remained confusing to a lot of people.[2]

Perhaps Malcolm X's greatest contribution to society was not his platform of militancy or nationalism or even black power, but rather his understanding that a truly free people, will go to great lengths to demonstrate and attain their freedom by any means necessary. "Power in defense of freedom is greater than power on behalf of tyranny and oppression," he said. "Because power, real power, comes from our conviction which produces action, uncompromising action." However, the king of Nationalism went to his grave too soon for our understanding. We wish we could say with so many others, "Long live the king."

1   Cone, James. H. *Martin & Malcolm & America: A Dream or a Nightmare*. Maryknoll, NY: Orbis Books, 1991, pg. 53

2   Ibid., pg. 4

A FOCUSED KING

After the Bus Boycott in Montgomery, Alabama, King became focused! He was so focused on his higher calling of leading black people out of their horrors of segregation and racism in America he resigned from his church. He then saw himself as a national and international leader. He had to focus on three main campaigns for the rest of his life: (1) the Civil Rights Struggle; (2) the War in Vietnam; and (3) the War on Poverty.

Those careful about his legacy say the $120 million monument to him that was constructed on the National Mall is an excellent tribute to King. As the nation commemorates his birth, some say he should best be remembered for his career-long focus on the poor.

A year before his 1968 death in Memphis, in his book, *Where Do We Go From Here? Chaos or Community,* King wrote: "I am now convinced that the simplest solution to poverty is to abolish it directly by a now widely discussed measure: the guaranteed income." His ideology was later to be expressed through his last campaign, the Poor Peoples Campaign. The idea was to guarantee that no one lived in poverty by having the government provide a financial floor, create a median, and set it where no incomes would fall beneath that median. King often talked about the psychological benefits of a widespread sense of "economic security." Economists John Kenneth Galbraith and Milton Friedman endorsed the idea of guaranteed incomes, as did Lyndon Johnson's Labor Secretary and later New York Sen. Daniel P. Moynihan. However, advocating and getting acceptance of the proposal was the official debate.

The Southern Christian Leadership Conference organized on November 27, 1967, the Poor People's Campaign to address issues of economic justice and housing for the poor in the United States, aiming itself at rebuilding America's cities. Martin Luther King and the Poor People's Campaign did not focus on just poor black people, but issued a safety net for all poor people. Martin Luther King, Jr., labeled the Poor People's Campaign the "second phase," of the civil rights struggle, setting goals such as gathering activists to lobby Congress for an "Economic Bill of Rights." Dr. King also saw a serious need to confront a Congress that had demonstrated its "hostility to the poor" and gave "military funds with alacrity and generosity," but provided "poverty funds with miserliness." Martin Luther King, Jr., was focused again on the oppressed.

Under the " Economic Bill of Rights" the Poor People's Campaign asked for the federal government to step it up in helping the poor with an antipoverty package that included housing and a guaranteed annual income for all Americans. King and other civil rights leaders planned the Poor People's Campaign in Washington, D.C., for the spring of 1968. The group decide to demand that President Lyndon Johnson and Congress help the poor get jobs, health care, and decent homes. To King, this was the bare minimum.

It was the intent of King and his organizers to make sure the campaign was going to be a peaceful gathering of poor people from communities across the nation. They wanted to march through Washington, D.C., the capital and visit numerous federal agencies in hopes of getting Congress to pass antipoverty legislation. They planned to stay in the city until some action was taken. Martin Luther King, Jr., announced the Poor People's Campaign at a staff retreat for the Southern Christian Leadership Conference in November 1967. Seeking a middle ground between riots on one hand and timid supplications for justice on the other," King planned for an initial group of 2,000 poor people to descend on Washington, D.C. In King's thought, southern states and northern cities could meet with government officials to demand those jobs, unemployment insurance, a fair minimum wage, and education for poor adults and children that were designed to improve their self-image and self-esteem.

The Poor People's Campaign was seen by King as the next chapter in the struggle for equality. Desegregation and the right to vote were essential, but King understood that Negroes and other minorities would never enter full citizenship until they had economic security. Through nonviolent direct action, King and SCLC hoped to focus the nation's attention on economic inequality and poverty. 'This is a highly significant event,' King told delegates at an early planning meeting, describing the campaign as 'the beginning of a new cooperation, understanding, and a determination by poor people of all colors and backgrounds to assert and win their right to a decent life and respect for their culture and dignity.'

Some members in the SCLC thought King's campaign too ambitious, and the demands too great. Although King praised the simplicity of the campaign's goals, saying, "it's as pure as a man needing an income to support his family,' he knew that the campaign was different from others that SCLC had attempted. Yet, he was focused on this last campaign for economic justice saying, 'We have an ultimate goal of freedom, independence, self-determination, whatever we want to call it, but we aren't going to get all of that now, and we aren't going to get all of that next year.' This he stated at a staff meeting on January 17, 1968. 'Let's do something that is so possible, so achievable, so pure, so simple that even the backlash can't do much to deny it. Yet, something so non-token and so basic to life that even the black nationalists can't disagree with it that much.' King knew that in response to black rioting in a number of cities during the summer of 1967, that convinced him, "The riot is the language of the unheard...America has failed to hear...that the promises of freedom and justice have not been met." Economic inequities were the next target for the movement.

In organizing this economic summit and movement, the Southern Christian Leadership Conference had designed a carefully detailed strategy for a sustained effort that would train poor people in the techniques of "militant nonviolence." Many other leaders representing American Indian, Puerto Rican, Mexican American, and poor white communities pledged themselves to the goals of the Poor People's Campaign. The means was to create a nonviolent uprising, a multiracial coalition of poor people and their allies who would march to Washington, D.C., set up mass encampments, and then launch protests every day until they achieved economic justice and equality.

KING'S FOCUSED IDEA ORIGINATED

In 1965 and 1966, King decided to extend organizing insights of the SCLC to the slums of Chicago to confront the evils of racist landlords. He moved his own family into the ghetto and a rundown housing unit in Chicago's famous Lawndale slum, where the family stayed for a time. King wanted to experience firsthand and demonstrate the devastation of poverty and overcrowding that other slum residents had endured for decades.

King and the SCLC organized huge marches for fair housing, and conducted systematic rent strikes where residents of many dilapidated buildings got together, refused to pay rent to the slumlords, and instead, collected their rent money to make building repairs. King was aware he had now crossed the line with capitalism's central decree that property rights were sacred.

There were long months of training in the discipline of

nonviolence. The Poor People's Campaign would march on Washington, D.C., erect shantytowns near the White House to make poverty visible, and then begin a campaign of massive sit-ins at federal agencies. The initial month of the campaign, thousands of poor people of all races came to shantytown. More than 6,000 soon came to the location better known as "The City of Hope" or "Resurrection City." King openly declared that his call for massive civil disobedience was aimed at disrupting, and ultimately paralyzing, the functions of the most powerful government on earth, until it granted the Economic Bill of Rights.

King understood that the shantytowns would make the suffering of economic deprivation so visible that federal legislators and the public would be forced to see it all around them in Washington, D.C. Then, once these encampments were known, they would force all America to confront the national disgrace of joblessness and poverty. King also had a stage two in mind, which would include a more militant phase of nonviolent resistance.

His words were visionary, uncompromising, revolutionary, and focused: "The dispossessed of this nation's poor, both white and black, live in a cruelly unjust society. They must organize a revolution against that injustice, not against the lives of their fellow citizens, but against the structures through which the society is refusing to lift the load of poverty."

If the president and Congress still refused to take actions to relieve poverty, the Poor People's Campaign would organize groups of protesters who would cause "major massive dislocations" at government buildings. Unemployed people would nonviolently block the Department of Labor and like institutions. Those without health care would be organized to sit in at hospitals and refuse to leave until they received medical treatment. Massive demonstrations would be held at federal agencies, while across the nation, allies would mount economic boycotts and nonviolent shutdowns of factories, manufacturing companies, and industries which refused to hire the poor.

Federal officials and the FBI held deep concerns over King's action and feared the direction he was taking. King announced the organization's intentions to lead a campaign of civil disobedience on a scale that could disrupt the nation's Capitol, and they denounced King totally. All of a sudden, there were those in opposition starting slanderous leaks, misinformation, and informants who were enlisted to discuss both King's and the organization's most private conversations. The government knew that being provocative were just some of the tools they needed to derail King's effort. Mr. Hoover and his team of FBI agents were on high alert.

King developed a strategy to confront the federal government with the same winnable dilemma earlier perfected by civil rights activists in Alabama, Georgia, and Mississippi: Either arrest innocent and poverty-stricken people by the thousands in the face of the nation and thereby create a national scandal, or submit to the just demands of those calling for an Economic Bill of Rights. The Poor People's Campaign held firm to the movement's commitment to nonviolence. "We are custodians of the philosophy of non-violence," King said at a press conference. "And it has worked." King had predicted that the Poor People's Campaign would be a turning point in American history, a chance for the nation to redeem itself from too long engrained poverty, racism, war, and exploitation.

Martin Luther King, Jr., had to be focused more on the Poor People's Campaign than he was during the Montgomery Boycott, or the written letter in a Birmingham Jail, or even when delivering his "I Have a Dream Speech" in Washington. This attack on economic injustice took every strength out of his mind, body, and soul. King predicted that attacking poverty would be much more difficult than earlier civil rights campaigns.

On June 25, 1967, King gave a speech at Victory Baptist Church in Los Angeles. "We aren't merely struggling to integrate a lunch counter now," he said. "We're struggling to get some money to be able to buy a hamburger or a steak when we get to the counter." The struggle for economic equality would cost a lot more than the fight to defeat Jim Crow segregation. Martin knew it didn't cost the nation one penny to integrate lunch counters. It didn't cost the nation one penny to guarantee the right to vote. The problems that they were facing then would cost the nation billions of dollars. What was needed, King said, was "a radical redistribution of economic and political power." King's critics had long been calling him a communist. King knew his demand for the redistribution of wealth would draw their fire. Yet, King was totally focused!

African-Americans started rioting in the poor neighborhoods of Detroit and Newark. King blamed poverty for fueling black anger. He called for a bold plan to help the nation's poor. When President Lyndon Johnson declared a "war on poverty" in 1964, he launched aggressive antipoverty initiatives. King believed Johnson's "Great Society" programs were being destroyed by the large sums going to the war in Vietnam.

King ultimately sent a long telegram to Johnson, urging

him to get rid of unemployment or risk greater urban unrest. King's telegram had no apparent effect on Johnson. In response, King waited long and hard for Johnson to retreat, but to no avail.

He soon announced the Poor People's Campaign to the media. In his letter, he said, "The Southern Christian Leadership Conference will lead waves of the nation's poor and disinherited to Washington, D.C., next spring to demand redress of their grievances by the United States government and to secure at least jobs or income for all. We will go there, we will demand to be heard and we will stay until America responds. If this means forcible repression of our movement, we will confront it, for we have done this before. If this means scorn or ridicule, we embrace it, for that is what America's poor now receive. If it means jail, we accept it willingly, for the millions of poor already are imprisoned by exploitation and discrimination... In short, we will be petitioning our government for specific reforms and we intend to build militant, nonviolent actions until the government moves against poverty."

King was very adamant about this new and innovative campaign on poverty. He told the congregation at Ebenezer Baptist Church in Atlanta, "Now I don't know about you, but I'm going to Washington to collect." After being held in slavery for 244 years, King said, African-Americans were set free in 1863, "Yet they were not given any land to make that freedom meaningful." King repeated this speech at mass rallies for the Poor People's Campaign across the country. He tried to infuse these rallies with hope instead of despair. He told numerous crowds, "Poverty is nothing new. What is new is that we now have the techniques and resources to get rid of poverty."

However, King never made it back to Shantytown. He was killed five days after he delivered the sermon at the National Cathedral. As organizers from cities in urban and rural areas strategized and gathered supplies, Martin Luther King, Jr., was assassinated on April 4, 1968.

THE OUTCOME OF A FOCUSED KING

Since King's death some forty-plus years ago, a movement to guarantee an income plan is being reawakened in academic and antipoverty circles as the nation looks at 15.3 million people seeking work with the prediction that large-scale and long-term unemployment will continue into the coming years. Organizations like the Basic Income Guarantee movement (USBIG.net) believe that increased mechanization and labor efficiencies, along with the export of industrial and manufacturing jobs to low-wage countries will lead to further joblessness and not enough work available. With the expansion of robotic technology and its potential to soon interpret and understand speech, even more jobs in the service industries will disappear. Yet, people will still need to live even without work.

King's dream of a nation without poverty will only come about with the creation of some antipoverty program funding for direct subsidization of adequate incomes which would solve some of the poverty problem while stimulating consumption. The University of Tennessee-Knoxville sociology professor, Harry F. Dahms, a member of the U.S. Basic Income Guarantee Network, says when he talks about the idea in the South, "audiences seem rather baffled, first, that such an idea even exists." Their second response is surprise "that some people would entertain it seriously."

In a class on social justice and public policy, Dahms, originally from Germany, discusses guaranteed incomes as a way for the work force to take advantage of growing efficiencies by having more people work fewer hours.

In Memphis, where Dr. King was assassinated, there are

efforts to enact a living wage for Shelby County and city employees and contractors were a step in the direction, of raising the income bar. Notwithstanding, Rebekah Jordan Gienapp, director of the Workers Interfaith Network, said King's call for raising the minimum wage to a level that could raise working people out of poverty would not be a partial solution. She noted that, adjustments for inflation are lower now than in 1968. Tennessee and Mississippi don't have state minimum wage laws and the minimum in Arkansas is lower than the current federal minimum wage. "What does that tell us about how we've really, in many ways, moved backwards since the civil rights movement in some of these economic ways?" she asks. "Particularly on Dr. King's birthday, he tends to be held up as just someone who advocated diversity or integration, but his message was much broader and more radical than that..."

Supporters of a guaranteed income acknowledge the solution sounds radical, but point to the subsidy every citizen of Alaska receives each year from the state's oil revenue. The share-the-wealth program is one of the most popular that efforts to repeal it have failed.

In closing this chapter, you would think King's suggestion on ending poverty in America would be an easy one. After all, America is still one of the richest nations in the world, in spite of its deficits. Many think that redistribution from the rich to the poor is the solution. Yet, to force people who have to give to the have-nots may, in fact, be a violation to a capitalistic country. Furthermore, to create a total welfare state would not be the sole solution as it may create the dependent poor.

I think what King was espousing to solve the poverty problem in America was to merely extend a fair opportunity to all. What may have been the problem was not only the issue of racism, but also classism and sexism. Once we get rid of some of these "isms," America may be able to get rid of it's poverty issue.

I think the problem exists because the Civil Rights and Voting Rights Bill did not do all they were intended to do which was to get rid of much of the discrimination in this nation. However, a focused King attempted to get America to begin thinking about economic injustice and economic empowerment. Unfortunately, beginning a campaign is not the same as seeing the end to that campaign. Many of King's ideologies went to the grave with him.

Chapter Nine
THE KING IS UNINTERRUPTED

While Martin Luther King, Jr., was solely focused on his campaign to liberate Negroes in America through nonviolent methods, Malcolm X's movement was a distraction for this man of peace. Malcolm constantly threw verbal jabs at King. The movement entrusted to Malcolm by the Honorable Elijah Muhammad, the Nation of Islam, was doing extremely well in serving blacks up north and around the country who bought into Black Nationalism philosophy as defined by Elijah. However, King, as told in previous chapters, moved his movement to a scale unprecedented by any other at the time.

Malcolm was constantly calling King negative names. While King saw America as "a dream...as yet unfulfilled," Malcolm viewed America as a "nightmare," as James Cone discussed in his book, *Martin & Malcolm & America: A Dream or a Nightmare*. Malcolm's life only served as a distraction from the attention Martin was receiving. Malcolm and his fear tactics dissuaded many blacks, especially those in the North, from adhering to or even hearing out King's nonviolent proposals for resolving the race issue. It was the intent of Malcolm to deny all truth to King's approach to America's dilemmas and to distract and dissemble his directives to civil and human rights issues in America.

It appeared that Malcolm's movement was to serve as a distraction and interruption to what the real King was doing. King was standing up for justice far differently than Malcolm and making far more progress in an era of challenge. King was prepared for his work having the luxury of academic tools not availed to Malcolm in prison. King was trained in the black experience and crossed over into the white American experience in his academic years at Crozer and Boston University. He had wrestled with his theories and had some of the greatest scholars of his day to challenge his thoughts and to evaluate his writings. King did so well in working out his sociology, politics, and religion that he was able to write them out in a book while vacationing. When it was time to act out on his theories he needed no more formal classes, only the school of the real world. King avoided moments when he could have met with the militant Malcolm X because he was aware that he could not afford the interruption or distraction. Although King knew Malcolm was one of his greatest critics, he refused to answer even his lesser critics believing that this would take too much of his most precious moments in life.

History only records one time when these two men met personally. It was on March 26, 1964, during a U.S. Senate debate on the Civil Rights bill. The Reverend Dr. Martin Luther King, Jr., was leaving a news conference that afternoon when Malcolm X stepped out of the crowd and blocked his path. According to a CNN report, Martin Luther King, Jr., extended his hand and smiled. "Well, Malcolm, good to see you," he said. "Good to see you," Malcolm X replied as both men broke into huge grins while a troop of photographers snapped pictures of their only meeting.

For the first and only time, the two kings, Martin Luther King, Jr., of Integrationism and Malcolm X of Nationalism, found themselves in the palace of Washington, D.C. While Malcolm was physically taller than King, King somehow loomed taller in his direction, stance, and solutions to the Civil Rights issues that would later prove to be true with the passage of the Civil Rights Act.

It is true that both men were instrumental in instilling

pride and confidence in the black community. However Martin Luther King, Jr., fought more for the civil rights movement than Malcolm X. He did it with grace and dignity, and in a nonviolent manner. He loved all races and wanted everyone to live together in peace. He knew he was going to be killed for his beliefs as Andrew Young would later reveal in interview after interview. Yet, he kept up the fight so that everyone could have equal rights. King remains to this day one of the most influential people in American history, towering over the accomplishments of Malcolm X.

To the majority of older white Americans and even many African-Americans today, the leadership and accomplishments of both Malcolm X and Dr. Martin Luther King, Jr., were as different from each other as night is from day. Mainstream culture and many history textbooks still suggest that the moderate Dr. King preached nonviolence and interracial harmony, whereas the militant Malcolm X advocated racial hatred and armed confrontation. Even Malcolm's famous slogan, "By Any Means Necessary!", still evokes among whites disturbing images of hatred and violence, armed shoot-outs, and disturbing urban insurrection.

But to the majority of Black Americans and to millions of whites under thirty, these two Black figures are now largely perceived as being fully complimentary with each other. Both leaders favored the building of strong Black institutions and healthy communities; both strongly denounced black-on-black violence and drugs within the urban ghetto; both aggressively opposed America's war in Vietnam and embraced the global cause of human rights. In a 1989 "dialogue" between the eldest daughters of these two assassinated Black heroes, Yolanda King and Attallah Shabazz, both women emphasized the fundamental common ground and great admiration the two men shared for each other, though we must remember that both of them were children at the time and seldom saw their fathers as frequently as other children.

However, Shabazz complained, "Playwrights always make Martin so passive and Malcolm so aggressive that those men wouldn't have lasted a minute in the same room." Yolanda King concurred, observing that in one play, "My father was this wimp who carried a Bible everywhere he went, including to someone's house for dinner." King argued, "That's not the kind of minister Daddy was! All these [are] ridiculous clichés." Both agreed that the two were indeed great men and leaders who were united in the pursuit of Black freedom and equality.

Somehow, I still see Martin standing taller than Malcolm even if it is by but an inch.

By the end of the turbulent sixties, for the generation of African-American students at overwhelmingly white college campuses, it was Malcolm X, not Dr. King, who became the greater symbol for the challenging civil rights period. Perhaps, to them he was the king of the voice for equality with his violent rhetoric. Although it is true that Malcolm X was perhaps one of the Black Power generation's greatest prophets and representatives, who spoke the uncomfortable truths that no one else had the courage or integrity to do, especially for young Black males. He personified for them everything they wanted to become as the embodiment of Black masculinity, authority, power, and uncompromising bravery in the face of racial oppression. Malcolm became the ebony standard for what the African-American liberation movement should be about. Working class Black people widely loved Brother Malcolm for what they perceived as his clear and direct style of language, and his peerless ability in making every complex issue "plain."

However, we must admit that the man who had been born Malcolm Little, transitioned to Malcolm X, and who had perished as El-Hajj Malik El-Shabazz was no saint. Though Malcolm was gifted, he was at the same time misguided. He made many serious errors of judgment, several of which directly contributed to his murder and the confusing of many blacks. Considering his last year in life, he admits that he had been wrong on many of the issues in the Black Power movement which led thousands and perhaps generations astray. During the last year of his life, he was dethroned as the black leader of the masses, yet enthroned as the attempted interracial leader for all.

What makes Martin Luther King, Jr., much more powerful is that he was consistent. He did not allow Malcolm to interrupt his thoughts on integration. King constantly stayed clear of Malcolm's presence and angry voice. Although he asked Coretta occasionally what she had heard Malcolm saying about him, I think the question was asked in passing. King kept the focus on his nonviolent movement. However, I think the only time King was really disturbed by Malcolm's ideology was when Malcolm accused King of not knowing anything about Black Power to which King responded, Black Power is just as dangerous as White Power. The real King was standing up!

Although I like Martin Luther King, Jr., I admire Malcolm X as a courageous leader. Even when he discovered he was wrong in black nationalist thoughts, he had the courage to admit it and change to the Orthodox Islamic faith and share his new views with the world.

With such an opinion of Malcolm, I in no way am diminishing Martin's accomplishments and courage. He spearheaded a movement that galvanized the nation. His name is iconic among great American leaders of all color. We now have a holiday, streets, boulevards, and a statue in his honor.

However, in a sense, Martin's path was "easier" in the beginning. He was raised in a Christian family. His father was a respected and loved pastor. His path was clear; his duty was to live according to his Christian conscience. His calling was as a pastor, and the civil rights movement needed leaders. He was there with the right skills, the compassion, the conviction, and the rhetorical ability at the right time. As a general in the Christian army, he knew he was on the winning side of the masses.

Malcolm's path was very different and much tougher. His childhood was rougher; he learned early that survival trumped any cause. He was a lost soul, the antithesis of Martin's peaceful resistance; he epitomized what the establishment feared in the black race. He rejected the American culture. In prison, he learned of the Black

Muslims' way. He found a societal paradigm that explained his life experience. His leadership finally found a positive outlet. He transformed, he submitted, he disciplined himself to give up alcohol, drugs, and fornication. Whereas Martin had to live according to his well-formed conscience, Malcolm had to create his conscience in a way that he could live it.

If Martin's message was "treat me as you would like to be treated," Malcolm's was "treat me as I deserve to be treated." Martin had the common ground of Christianity to relate to white America. Malcolm's embracing of Islam was just another thumbing of his nose at the establishment. He could no more negotiate with America than he could negotiate with his own intellectual integrity. This integrity issue is what forced his next transformation.

Up to this point, his leadership was already forcing people to address uncomfortable ideas. He kept searching, making his pilgrimage to Mecca, and at last realizing the true brotherhood of humanity. He rediscovered that the God of power and the God of love was the same God. He submitted again, upsetting his position in the Nation of Islam, irritating the hierarchy, dooming his life to become a martyr to truth.

In high school, I read *The Autobiography of Malcolm X*, and perhaps it was just my age, but I was at a place on my own path which allowed his story to resonate deeply in my heart and mind. Martin Luther King, Jr., was so well known and idolized, it was sometimes hard to consider him as a mere man. It probably seemed like blasphemy to even consider another black leader. Malcolm X pushed things more, and the more he upset people, the more he changed people's identities. Picturing him with his Fruit of Islam bodyguards was an impressive display of the power of self-determination.

In a backhanded way, Martin's success and stature were due to Malcolm's mistakes and mishaps. As uncomfortable as Martin made the white establishment feel, he seemed reasonable compared to Malcolm. If the times they lived were changing, at least Martin represented a change in a stable direction, towards a new America where whites and blacks could both be happy. Martin began to loom taller than Malcolm. However, Malcolm didn't care about happiness. If both were still alive, I think they would still be fighting separate fights. There is plenty of struggle still left, and plenty of room for both. Although Martin seemed more contemporary, his ideals still ring true. Malcolm's seemed more time limited. Malcolm could have been an ambassador to the emerging African states, but not an ambassador to America.

Chapter Ten
WHEN TWO KINGS ARE DEAD

MALCOLM IS DEAD

Malcolm X influenced many of the leaders who sought to give guidance to the militancy of the Black Power era. However, his intellectual legacy did not bridge the divide between black leaders and totally mobilize black masses. Shortly after Malcolm X was assassinated, his militancy died with him. He stood as the king of black nationalism during his time, but the nationalist king's platform and throne crumbled quickly, even as Elijah Muhammad and Louis Farrakhan attempted to maintain its royalty.

Despite his rhetorical support for black militancy, Malcolm himself did not lead a protest or insurgent movement. Indeed, Malcolm's principal contribution to the black nationalist tradition was to link that tradition with the mass movements of his time. Therefore, his movement was time limited. As Malcolm observed the intensifying civil rights demonstrations of 1963 and 1964, he moved from harsh criticisms of nonviolence and integrationism to a more subtle review that distinguished between national and civil rights leaders. Although Malcolm continued to challenge King and other established civil rights leaders, he also became increasingly critical of the Nation of Islam's apolitical orientation: "I felt that, wherever black people committed themselves, in the Little Rocks and the Birminghams and other places, militantly disciplined Muslims should also be there for all the world to see, and respect, and discuss." This could not be the position of an Honorable Elijah Muhammad who was accused of child molestation that could have ended him in jail.

It could be heard increasingly in the Negro communities: Those Muslims talk tough, but they never do anything, unless somebody bothers a Muslim. By the time of the March on Washington, Malcolm combined attacks on national black leaders, stating, "they control you, but they have never incited you or excited you," with generous praise for "local leaders," who had begun "to stir up our people at the grass-roots level."

After leaving the Nation of Islam, Malcolm formed the Organization of Afro-American Unity (OAAU) and began reaching out to militant leaders. In October 1964, while on a tour of Africa, he met with SNCC representatives, persuading them to cooperate with his newly established group. In December, he hosted Fannie Lou Hamer and other leaders at a Harlem OAAU meeting and met with a delegation of teenagers from the McComb, Mississippi, movement. During February 1965, he traveled to Selma, Alabama, to address young voting rights activists. While there, he attempted to meet with Martin Luther King, Jr., but because the civil rights leader was in jail, he assured Coretta Scott King of his desire to help the civil rights struggle. By the time of his assassination on February 21, Malcolm's different kind of black nationalism emphasized militant political engagement rather than racial-religious separatism. Before his death, he changed!

Many of Malcolm's followers continued to quote his speeches as minister of the Nation of Islam, the group whose leaders condemned Malcolm as a traitor "worthy of death." After his death, most followers gave more attention to Malcolm's criticisms of civil rights leaders than to his efforts to forge ties with activists. They gave more focus to his racial ideas than to his political thought. Malcolm's intellectual legacy became a different set of ideas that had both conservative and radical implications, ideas that encouraged generalized pessimism about the future as well as revolutionary enthusiasm. The king of nationalism, Malcolm X, now seemed to have been set on the outskirts of his kingdom. He had become too confusing and did not have enough time in life to clarify his positions even with himself.

Black power advocates, such as Stokely Carmichael and H. Rap Brown, and Black Panther leaders popularized Malcolm's brand of rhetorical militancy, but they had little success in building a real politically effective mass movement. Black Power militancy produced lasting ideological and cultural contributions, but it also created destructive ideological and cultural conflicts within the black militant community. Intending to create a unified and revolutionary black movement, black power advocates instead competed with one another to determine which ideas should become the basis of racial unity and who should become its next leader. Their ideas were not long lasting in the African-American community nor in the broader community. Could it be that they were the ones responsible for dethroning the king and his ideology during and after Malcolm's death?

In retrospect, the assassination of Malcolm X can be seen as the prototype of subsequent deadly and demoralizing black-against-black crimes that made black militancy more vulnerable to external manipulation and extinction. Rather than serving as "intellectuals" building on the emergent ideas of the later years of Malcolm X and of the ongoing struggles, some Black Power proponents, if ideological conversion and cultural training were necessary preconditions for effective racial struggle, arrogantly sought to "raise" the black masses to a higher level of consciousness. They clearly did not understand the new Malcolm's narrowly conceived, purist, or "blacker than thou" ideological philosophies that were intended to unify African-Americans, but which instead, divided them. Black ideologues, without real thought, competed for the role of the black "messiah," who, in the mind of FBI director, J. Edgar Hoover, could "unify and electrify the militant black nationalist movement." Their height in history toppled as well. Unfortunately, Malcolm X did not go far enough in getting a mass America accepting of his leadership and was set down by the system and dethroned by his own selfish subjects and leaders in the Nation of Islam starting with his mentor, the Honorable Elijah Muhammad.[1]

MALCOLM IS DEAD, BUT THE KING LIVES ON

The ideas of Martin Luther King, Jr., and Malcolm X (who died first) have become far better known to the current generation of African-American and American youth than have the organizing techniques that made possible the Civil Rights era's grassroots movements.

King and Malcolm have become larger than life icons and great men who were agents of historical change rather than products of their time.

These two male icons have become far more widely known for changing the course of African American history than all of the other Civil Rights leaders collectively. Contemporary black youth are likely to see King and Malcolm as representing opposing ideological positions rather than seeing Malcolm as offering partial, incomplete insights into fundamental issues of the African-American experience. However, King's ideology of integration and the unity of the American masses and the American dream lives on even today.

In a recent article by *USA Today* titled, "Martin Luther King's Legacy Still Lives On," the writer suggests that King's legacy can be expressed in one sentence: Epic changes can be made without carrying a gun. Martin loved the timeless ethics of Jesus of the New Testament, and people everywhere still embrace them. Dr. King helped transform a nation and in Washington his monument lines up with the Lincoln and Jefferson memorials. Today, the conversations are about inclusiveness, cultural plurality, ethnicities, and the spirit of freedom.

On the National Mall in Washington, Martin Luther King, Jr., is a towering, heroic figure carved in a 30-foot-tall sculpture emerging as a "stone of hope" hewn out of a "mountain of despair."

Some gaze upon King's monument in silence. Others smile and pull out their cell phones and cameras and shout, "We are here with the big King." Some watch and observe him from the sole of his shoes to the top of his head. Others sit thinking, what more can we do behind the Prince of Peace? Still others stand in companies of two or three wondering what more can we do to re-inspire the great movement he started? Yet another stands in front of the monument, wondering if we will ever know the real Martin Luther King, Jr.? Will the real King stand up?

1 Carson, Clayborne. Malcolm X: The FBI File (USA: Skyhorse Publishing, 2012), pg. 39.

CONCLUSION

At the conclusion of this book, we still have an outstanding question: Why this book, at this time? Why this debate on who is the real King?

When President George W. Bush was in office standing up for war in Iraq, many took to the streets to protest his policies. The resistance to the war on Iraq and then Afghanistan produced a major antiwar movement with heightened consciousness that developed faster and with a sharper focus than the movement against the Vietnam War.

We saw the formation of modern day Martin Luther Kings who stood up recreating the Civil Rights leader's: "We cannot fight two wars at one time: a War in Iraq and a War on Poverty."

We still need the spirit of King embodied in each of our

lives to fight against injustice anywhere because, as King stated, "an injustice anywhere is a threat to justice everywhere."

Now we have the Obama moment. He eliminated Bush's war, yet he extended it into Libya, and we have no real antiwar movement challenging Obama's legitimacy. The ruling class is using a Black man to advance the cause of neoliberalism. They are concerned more about bailing out banks "too big to fail" than unemployment and the suffering of masses of people who are falling by the wayside.

Maybe I should say Obama is our man doing America's work, and he is standing up in the stead of King. History is yet to be written on our president. In his speeches, he often sounds like King. Many Americans voted for him a second time, but many are questioning whether he has the courage to fight for us.

Rather than give us the Malcolm X of the Detroit Speeches, the Malcolm X we think we know, I want to give you the remade Malcolm. It may seem as if I have cut him down to size with unsubstantiated arguments under the guise of trying to humanize Malcolm X. However, history bears it out that unfortunately he was cut down too soon and never became an old man to learn what his ultimate direction for this nation would have been.

In summary, I've tried to give you a perspective that is not only within the confines of the Black studies tradition, but the American way. I hope I have not just created another King book you can place in your library. I did not want to fabricate a Malcolm who was just a militant and a Martin who was merely an integrationist. I hope you seriously looked at one of them, King, who fortunately lived long enough to work out his perspectives and gave us a real model of change for proven paradigms to eliminate both war and poverty. That's the reason for this book, at this time.

BIBLIOGRAPHY

Baker, Houston. *Betrayal: How Black Intellectuals have Abandoned the Ideals of the Civil Rights Era.* New York: Columbia University Press, 2008.

Clarke, John Henrik, ed. *William Styron's Nat Turner: Ten Black Writers Respond.* Boston: Beacon Press, 1968.

Cone, James. H. *Martin & Malcolm & America: A Dream or a Nightmare.* Maryknoll, NY: Orbis Books, 1991

Douglass, Frederick. *The Life and Writings of Frederick Douglass, Volume 2.* Philip S. Foner, ed. New York, International Publisher, 1950.

Duberman, Martin Bauml. *Paul Robeson.* New York: Alfred A. Knopf, 1988.

Dyson, Michael Eric. *I May Not Get There With You: The True Martin Luther King, Jr.* New York: Free Press, 2000.

Engels, Frederick. *Translated by Emile Burns.* Moscow: Progress Publishers, 1947. Available at http:// www.marxists.org/archive/marx/works/1877/anti-duhring/

Garrow, David J. *Bearing the Cross: Martin Luther King, Jr., and the Southern Christian Leadership Conference.* New York: William Morrow & Company, 1986.

Lee, Spike. *Malcolm X [movie]*, 1992.

Marable, Manning. *Malcolm X: A Life of Reinvention.* New York: Viking, 2011.

Muhammad, Elijah. *How to Eat to Live, Volume 1.* Chicago, Muhammad Mosque of Islam No. 2, 1967. Available at http://www.seventhfam.com/temple/ books/ eattolive_one/eat1index.htm

Muhammad, Elijah. *How to Eat to Live, Volume 2.* Chicago, Muhammad Mosque of Islam No. 2, 1972. Available at http://www.seventhfam.com/temple/ books/ eattolive_two/eat2index.htm

Perry, Bruce. *Malcolm: The Life of a Man Who Changed Black America*. Barrytown, NY: Station Hill Press, 1991.

Sales, William W. *From Civil Rights to Black Liberation: Malcolm X and the Organization of Afro-American Unity*. Boston: South End Press, 1994.

Stanford, Maxwell C. "Revolutionary Action Movement (RAM): A Case Study of an Urban Revolutionary Movement in Western Capitalist Society." Master's thesis. Atlanta University, 1986. Available at http://www.ulib.csuohio.edu/research/portals/blackpower/stanford.pdf

Styron, William. *The Confessions of Nat Turner: A Novel*. New York: Random House, 1967. Williams, Robert F. Negroes with Guns. New York, Marzani & Munsell, 1962.

Wolfenstein, E. Victor. *The Victims of Democracy: Malcolm X and the Black Revolution*. Berkeley: University of California Press, 1981

Made in the USA
Charleston, SC
17 February 2014